The Won
Naval
a World War Two memoir

Brenda Birney

ISBN: 978-1-365-31556-5

Contents

Editor's Preface

Introduction

1. Joining the Women's Royal Naval Service – 1941

2. Dover 1942-3

3. 3rd Officer Heimann prepares for the Invasion of Normandy 1943-4

4. Italy 1945

5. Malta 1945

6. Invalided out 1946

Postscript

Editor's Preface

My mother, Brenda Birney must have first joined an Autobiography writing class when she was in her late 70's or early 80's. This was at U3A (University of the Third Age) in the old Hampstead Town Hall near Belsize Park underground station. She wrote about all periods of her life. Brenda always loved writing. She stopped attending the classes and writing when my father became very incapacitated. After his death at the age of 97 in 2008 she re-joined for a period.

A very competent shorthand typist, much of her life story would have been written on a manual typewriter. As a family we persuaded Brenda to transfer to using a PC. She never became accustomed to it. Some stories were written many times and saved page by page as separate, nameless files. Some were not entirely saved. There are hand-written pages and hand written amendments. I have had to select versions and fit some together to complete the jigsaw. I have edited as lightly as possible. The writing is all my mother's in which she recounts this part of her life as Wren rating and then 3rd Officer Heimann during the 2nd World War.

These were the stories upon which I grew up as a child and so even now they are very familiar. Some of Brenda's closest Wren friends were my "aunties" through childhood. Just recently I have met Mary Quarry's eldest son for the first time in 50 or more years! As a child I thought all these stories had happened long ago, in the Dark Ages. Only as an adult do I realise that I was born just three years after she left the Service and as soon as I could follow, say by the age of 7, she was telling me of her adventures.

The most exciting years of my mother's life were those serving in the WRNS. She wrote to be read......

Hazel Dakers, June 2016

Introduction

Brenda Heimann was born in Golders Green in NW London on 19th September 1917. Her father was serving in the trenches in Northern France. Her mother already had two little girls, Bernice (Bunny) born in 1914 and Maxine (Maxie) born in 1915.

Brenda's father was South African, a Jewish atheist, and her mother was from Liverpool of a Church of England background but apparently educated in a Quaker school or orphanage. Her mother was briefly "on the stage" and a model for a famous photographer of the Edwardian period, Elwin Neame. Her father had studied at what is now the University of Cape Town and then with other bright, young men of his time had travelled to England to take further degrees in Cambridge. He had inherited a large sum as a very small child. But he had lived it up until 1914 and there was very little left by the early 1920s. He volunteered for the British Army in the early days of the First World War rather than launching his intended career as a barrister. He never managed to practice after the War by which time he had changed from a fun-loving young man to a dour father of whom at least his two younger daughters were scared.

Brenda followed her sisters to Wessex Gardens Primary School. From there she moved to Hendon County. After two years her father was dissatisfied with her learning and transferred her to join her sisters at La Sagesse Convent School. After Matric he paid for Brenda to attend Pitmans Secretarial College. I think she always regretted not going to university. However, her father felt if he could not afford it for all his daughters that it was unfair to favour one. And so, it was as a secretary in a firm called Industrial Engineering[1] that she decided to volunteer for the WRNS.

Hazel Dakers, June 2016

---

[1] Brenda spoke equally of Industrial Engineering and Ralli Bros. I believe the former was a subsidiary of the latter.

1. Joining the Women's Royal Naval Service - 1941

By 1941 more and more men and women appeared on the streets in uniform but it was sometime before it hit me that maybe I should join one of the Forces. But once it had taken root in my brain I began to wonder if it would be feasible. Neither of my sisters was living at home and I wondered how my parents would feel about the last one leaving home. In a way I felt I would be letting them down. But it also seemed to me there were more important things at stake. We knew nothing about the concentration camps but we did know how badly the Jews were treated in Germany[2] and we also knew Germany had broken all international agreements and had marched into countries where they had no right to be. On top of all that, we were enduring air raids which no human beings should be expected to endure. Every day I wondered what devastation I would see on my way to work and stories of the terrible bombing in the East End continually arrived.

Not having any affiliation with any particular Service, I made a firm decision to apply first to the WRNS and if they refused me I'd try the WAAF, leaving the ATS till the last. I think it was the uniforms made me put them in that order. I knew nothing about the Navy but nor did I about the Air Force or the Army. None of my friends had joined up, nor as far as I knew had any intention of doing so. I decided I had dithered around long enough, so went along to HQ and offered my services. I was called for an interview for the WRNS when I was asked if I had any particular reason for wanting to join them. It didn't occur to me that the correct answer to this was that my father, uncle or whoever, was an admiral, although this did cross my mind much later[3].

---

[2] In fact, Brenda later acknowledged that her own mother's German friend Lily Weiss (who travelled in Germany in the 1930s but lived in England) warned of such things, as did the Left Book Club of which her friend (and eventual husband) Leo was a member.

[3] Brenda later noted by hand at the beginning of the 21st century, through her daughter's family history research, that there was indeed in the family Admiral Hill-Norton - a distant cousin of ours and last Admiral of the Fleet - with whom her daughter was in touch in the last years of his life. During WW2 he was a gunnery officer. 1971-4 he was Chief of the Defence Staff and in 1977 Chairman of the Military Committee of NATO.

I simply told them that I felt I should be doing my share towards the war effort (standard answer) and that I was prepared to join any of the women's Services (not such a clever answer). Despite this, they accepted me. It was now the end of 1941 and I was told to present myself at Westfield College in Hampstead on 3rd February 1942[4].

On the whole my parents accepted it all very well, to my surprise neither trying to dissuade nor encouraging, which was a great relief to me. My father had volunteered for the Army in the Great War (as a South African he need not have joined up) and absolutely hated it. Mr Macey, my boss at Industrial Engineering where I then worked at Bush House, encouraged me. Mr Kelsey, the big white chief, tried to dissuade me. However, I had made up my own mind and was determined to go ahead with it. When the time came they each gave me a very nice leaving gift (one was a gold watch) and I promised to keep in touch by letter. My sister Bunny was satisfied with her Red Cross work. She had now formed a Junior Red Cross group at our old school, La Sagesse Convent. Anyway, she was now a Quaker and Quakers are always pacifists. My other sister Maxie, as far as I knew, had no yearnings that way. Our school friend Sonia tried to follow me but was turned down due to her Russian parentage. Former colleague at Industrial Engineering and close friend, Mollie later joined the Land Army, the Timber Corps, and I can't remember anyone else I knew joining any of the Services.

The 3rd February arrived all too soon. I didn't like to arrive at Westfield College, Hampstead, in a taxi. I thought it might create the wrong impression. Actually, had anyone seen me arrive, it would have created the right impression. As it was, as nobody took a blind bit of notice of me anyway, trudging up the icy road with my suitcase feeling as if it was packed with lead, I didn't create any impression at all.

It was the nearest I was ever to get to going to university. I suppose all the students had been evacuated to some bomb-free part of the country, or they'd joined up or something. Anyway, all I know is we had their college as our training centre. I was to be trained as a writer. That is, to work in an office. The fact that I had been working in an office for several years already made no difference. A training depot it was and trained I must be. I was the best in the writers' class. Most of the others had come straight from school. They looked on this as a crash course from which

---

[4] Brenda's service record indicates that on 3rd February 1942 she reported to Pembroke I (Westfield College) and that 16/17 February she was at Pembroke III (in Mill Hill).

we would emerge after three weeks as fully fledged secretaries.

I remembered the words of my boss's boss, Mr Kelsey, the Governing Director, "Don't join," he exhorted me, "the more secretaries they have, the more letters they'll write and the more of my time they'll waste reading them". Of course, I was terrified of him. But, even so, I could see he was hampering the war effort. If they needed to write letters to win, I would help them. I couldn't encourage him to be so selfish.

From the moment we went aboard Westfield College they did their utmost to let us know we were in the Navy. No more shilly-shallying around as miserable civvies; no more beds and bedrooms here at sea but bunks, cabins, decks and nutty. And sproggs, which we were.

We were five of us in our cabin. Four had to sleep in bunks and there was a bed (which mustn't be called a bed). Somehow it became mine. If the air raid warning went in the night, we were told, we must get up immediately and make our way to a corridor onto a floor below. We realised this would be simpler than remaining on the same floor as we would then be over crowded by the people making their way from another floor to our floor. Of course, the siren did go in the middle of the night and we all five did our best to follow instructions but, as Georgette explained to the 1st Officer later, in her fervour to be the first to rise and shine, she had overlooked the fact that she was on the upper bunk and came crashing to the floor. As none of us knew this wasn't a real air raid but simply an exercise through which they put all sproggs on their first night, we were torn between rushing to safety and leaving her there on the floor or staying until she regained consciousness. In the end we compromised: two of us took her head and two her feet and we lugged her to the head of the stairs. When she realised she had the choice between being dropped over the bannisters or coming to, she decided on the latter course. We all got a bottle over this as there was no excuse for being the last to appear. This upset us no end as we were all trying to make a good impression.

Being the best in my writers' class, I was chosen to rush to the rescue in the first emergency. I was proud. I had not yet been asked to sign the pledge nor indeed had I a uniform. But in their own way they told me how I'd be helping to save the country. That is, they told me to report to HMS "Lynx" in Dover immediately.

Brenda - Wren rating

2. Dover 1942-3

Once again I was on the move with my huge suitcase packed, it felt, with lead. I had been hastily fitted out with shirt and tie, over which I wore a navy blue stiff cotton overall, a raincoat and a small round, brimmed hat. The shirt had a separate stiff collar which rubbed my neck raw. Add to this thick black lisle stockings (no nylons in those days, nor tights) and flat heeled black lace-up shoes, and you may get the idea of the picture of elegant allure I presented. I had been too small to wear their smallest size in uniforms - you could have put two of me into the skirt alone, which reached to my ankles.

"There is no time to get it altered here" the 1st Officer told me, "get it done in Dover". A little shattered by the fact that I had chosen the WRNS partly because I'd look something of a dish in the uniform, I consoled myself with the thought that I was rushing to serve King and Country.

As the train pulled in at Dover Priory[5], a soldier asked me if I was going to the Wrennery.

"Dover College," I replied.

"That's only a wee step," he said, "can I carry your case for you?"

By the time he had heaved it down, he was red in the face and perhaps regretting his kind offer. By the time he had deposited it and me outside the front door of Dover College, our romance was over. He had gone by the time an officer leaped up the steps two at a time and said as she whizzed past,

"No ratings allowed in this way. Go round the side entrance."

My cabin was on the third floor. My case delayed my progress but eventually I got there. I opened the door to find a ravishing blonde brushing her hair in front of a mirror. Ever ready for the comradely word, I stood for a moment and looked at her. She neither glanced towards me nor acknowledged in any other way the fact that someone had walked in. While I was trying to pluck up the courage to break the silence and ask her which of the four bunks I was to occupy, she threw her gas mask over her shoulder and walked out.

I looked at myself in the mirror and felt depressed. However, after a

---

[5] WRNS service file records Brenda's arrival at Lynx, the Royal Naval base at Dover 18 February 1942.

few minutes I pulled myself together and decided I had better follow the instructions I had been given.

"Take the ferry to the Castle and report to Commander Ede in Minesweeping," I had been told.

I stood outside the College and wondered which way to go to find the sea and the ferry. A dark haired girl came over after a few minutes.

"Do you need any help?" she enquired.

It was such a relief they weren't all like the blonde upstairs, so I told her I had to catch the ferry to the Castle and I didn't know where to go.

"Oh," she said, "just wait here. It'll be along soon. If you see the driver is a fabulous raven haired beauty, wearing long boots up to her knees, that'll be Snow White. She's not awfully bright but if you tell her where you have to go, she'll drop you off there. By the way, my name's Miriam."

So I had learned something: a ferry did not necessarily float on water.

I couldn't mistake Snow White, with her pale skin and jet black hair. She really was lovely. I wondered how she got away with wearing these high boots instead of lace up shoes but didn't like to ask her. We went up a steep hill and, if I strained my neck, at certain turns I could just see the Castle above us. But we stopped before we reached it. Snow White pointed to what looked like the entrance to a cave.

"Walk straight through till you come to some people at desks. One of them will be Commander Ede," she said, starting the engine of her van again.

She had disappeared in a second, so I had no alternative but to penetrate the cave. In fact, it turned out not to be exactly a cave but a long tunnel. I had walked some distance before I saw anyone.

"Commander Ede?" I enquired of a young man approaching me. I couldn't even tell anyone's rank at this point. In fact, he turned out to be a sub-lieutenant RNVR (Royal Naval Volunteer Reserve).

"Oh, you must be our new Wren," someone bellowed out. "You live up there in the Crow's Nest."

A rough wooden staircase ran up to an equally rough looking hut hanging from the ceiling.

"Lieutenant Matthews will show you the ropes."

I climbed carefully up the steep stairs, hanging onto the bannister as I went, and I should say it was a miracle I didn't get any splinters in my hand.

"Oh, you're taking Miriam's place, are you?" said Lt Matthews.

Miriam? Miriam? I thought. Could that possibly be the Miriam who had told me about the ferry?

"Pat works in this office with me and yours is just through there."

The Crow's Nest only contained these two rooms. Mine had a bookshelf full of old, tatty thrillers.

"Those are for when you're not busy." Pat said. "Commander Ede will yell for you when he wants you. What's your Christian name?"

Pat went home at about five o'clock. She was one of a few Wrens who lived at home and came in daily. I had no idea of when I should leave. I asked Lieutenant Matthews.

"Well," he said, "Commander Ede usually has something for you at about seven o'clock. After you've done that, you can go."

By the time Cdr. Ede yelled for me, on the dot of seven, Lieutenant Matthews had also left.

Commander Ede dictated a weather report to me.

As the days passed by I found that the main part of my work consisted of four weather reports a day. In between I wrote letters to my parents, to my sisters, to my friends. This seemed ridiculous. Next time I saw Miriam she asked me if I liked the job!

"Have I taken your job?" I asked her.

"Well, er, yes, as a matter of fact."

I liked Commander Ede who, incidentally, was known as Commander "Bloody" Ede as every other word he used had this prefix. Sometimes if Pat and I were chatting he would shout, "Stop that bloody row up there!" Invariably this would be followed shortly afterwards by, "For God's sake, carry on. The bloody silence is worse than the bloody chatter!"

During this time I found my way around the Wrennery and Dover. The other girls in my cabin worked watches so we seldom met up. Many years later I met by chance Annetta[6] and for a while we became friends again. Notices went up frequently that the Marines or others were having a hop on a particular night and would like some Wrens to go. As always I loved to dance, so whenever anyone suggested it to me, I went.

I had not escaped the air raids when I left London; in fact, here we also had shelling as the Germans were now on the north coast of France from

---

[6] By then both were married, Annetta to the artist famous for his musical cartoons and crazy concerts, Gerard Hoffnung. Hazel remembers their mutual visits during her early childhood when the Hoffnungs lived nearby in Hampstead Garden Suburb.

where their guns could reach Dover. A shelling warning was a double air raid warning. I can remember a shell falling on civilians queuing for a bus in the main square in broad daylight. A number were killed I think. It was finally decided that Wrens working regular hours should be taken out of Dover before dark during the light periods, that is, when the moon lit up the town. And so it was when my turn came round to join those being taken to Poulton. It was an old and primitive smallpox hospital in the middle of the countryside. It consisted of two wards separated by a toilet and bathroom. Each ward had about twelve beds. There was only dim lighting, perhaps one candle or oil lamp. Each ward had a tall, round boiler in the middle which couldn't be used as there was no fuel. It was bitterly cold and snowing hard.

We later moved from Dover College to a village just outside Dover called Kearsney where a large house had been acquired for the WRNS. This meant we no longer had to escape during the light periods. I should think about 15-20 of us moved there with an Admin Officer, Mrs. Goddard, in charge. She was a pleasant woman, surprisingly shy, but who ran the quarters efficiently and we were all very happy there. As the spring and summer approached it was particularly enjoyable as it had a large garden. My parents even came to visit me. This was far pleasanter than Dover College and Poulton and I even went for a few shaky bicycle rides around the country.

My former colleagues at Industrial Engineering in Bush House were all very good about writing to me and Nina Sadler said her parents were living temporarily in Hythe, near Folkestone. The manager and manageress of a hotel there, fearful of the air raids, had left without warning and as the hotel belonged to her Father's firm, Mr. Sadler had volunteered to take over at least for the time being. Her mother had said any time I felt lonely I should visit them. Also, I would be hearing from another friend of hers who lived at Seabrook, also near there.

In due course I had a very charming letter from this lady asking me to let her know when I could pay her a visit. On the appointed day I arrived at a beautiful house on the top of the cliff. Mrs. Sylvester introduced me to her husband and then took me upstairs to her bedroom. It was a large room, elegantly decorated in shades of grey, and she invited me to take a seat in one of the comfortable armchairs. I thought in a little odd to entertain me in her bedroom but I sat down as requested and she produced from a drawer two books. One was the Bible and the other Mrs.

9

Baker Eddy's book on Christian Science.

Horror of horrors! What should I do? Religion played no part in our upbringing, our Father Jewish only by birth and my Mother being a non-practicing Christian. Mrs. Sylvester passed me Mrs. Baker Eddy's book.

"Let's go to page 56," she said, "you read first and then I'll read the passage from the Bible."

Obviously there had been some misunderstanding. Nina was a Christian Scientist and Mrs. Sylvester must think I was, too. You mustn't get the wrong idea. I admired their belief that illness could be cured by the mind but I wasn't quite sure that I believed it. But what should I do now? This lady had taken me into realms of religion I didn't want but I felt I couldn't say anything. Thank heavens, I was a reasonably good reader but with all this going on in the back of my mind I began to stumble. If only her husband would come in or the 'phone would ring or anything to bring this to an end. I should have told her right away but I didn't. What should I do now? How stupid I was!

At last she said, "Shall we take a break now and have a cup of tea?"

I looked at my watch.

"That would be lovely," I said, "and then I shall have to go."

I finally asked for a transfer from Minesweeping. I decided they could not object to my wanting a job with more work and they quickly acquiesced. Thus I became a "floating" Wren[7] and was told I would take over where anyone was ill or absent for any other reason. I liked the idea as I felt I would get more variety. My first destination was HMS "Wasp" which was at the opposite end of Dover from the Castle. From the main square I had to walk down Snargate Street which I loved. It was an old road with lots of pubs and in the evening was full of drunken sailors. I don't know why but I was never nervous. Possibly it was because there were always plenty of people around.

HMS "Wasp" had been the Lord Warden Hotel before the war but was now a Coastal Base Force. Coastal Forces were made up of MTBs (motor torpedo boats). They were about 60 feet long and were manned by young and very brave men. MTBs were too small for bunks so "Wasp" a shore establishment, fulfilled that requirement. It was their base. Their work was to go out at night into the Channel to meet the German U-boats. I always felt it needed more courage and skill than the Air Force pilots who dropped bombs over Germany.

[7] WRNS service file records for 19 May 1942 Lynx HSR (Higher Specialised Rate)

One of the WRNS cooks, Sheila Forsyth, used to get up when the men were expected back in the night and make them sandwiches and cocoa. I helped her once and I well remember the cockroaches in the galley. I shudder at the thought even now. They were swarming over everything. Fortunately, no food was kept there. Sheila was so practical: she simply took a large cloth and wiped them off all the surfaces whilst I cowered in the doorway. (Incidentally she is still a friend of mine[8] living in Sutherland, the northernmost part of Scotland.)

After I had worked at HMS "Wasp" for a short time, it was suggested I should move in. The WRNS had quarters on the mezzanine floor. It seemed unlikely I would "float" anywhere else for the time being, so much as I liked living at Kearsney, I agreed. For some reason the Wrens at "Wasp" were not expected to go to Poulton during light periods, as were those based at HMS "Lynx" (Dover College), so that, too, was a consideration.

I shared a cabin with a girl named Pat Bailey and she and I got on very well together. I should think 10-15 of us lived at "Wasp". There was only one bathroom but, fortunately, many of them worked watches, so the demand for this was spread over the whole day. Some of us, too, had basins in our cabins with hot and cold running water. I was warned some of the seamen who used floors above us had made peepholes in the temporary wall of the bathroom which faced the staircase!

I worked in what is known in the Royal Navy as the Captain's Office. Between our office and the Captain's was that of his secretary, a Second Officer WRNS. We did all the work in our office and I have yet to decide what on earth she did in hers. Well, some things I knew but they were nothing to do with the running of "Wasp". The Captain was a rarity in the Navy as he was a lower deck Captain, in other words he had come from the non-commissioned ranks.

We were four or five of us in the Captain's Office. Firstly, there was Minnie Miller, who was a petty officer and the most senior of us. There were two girls who worked a printing machine and either one or two typists. All of us except Minnie were the lowest rank of Wren.

Minnie's job was to enter into a log book every piece of paper that entered into our office before it was passed on to the Captain whom Minnie liked to think was in love with her.

"Oh, you'll never guess the things he's been telling me," she would

---

[8] Sheila Turner, née Forsyth died in the early years of the 21st century

say, gleefully. "Of course, I can't tell any of you, they're too confidential."

"Oh, go on Minnie," the others would say.

I didn't need to say anything. I knew she had to tell someone. Invariably, as soon as we were alone she would say, "I can tell you, Brenda."

After a while I started to have a few problems myself with the Captain. First, he became incapable of signing a letter without holding my hand. I didn't quite know what to say so I said nothing, feeling it was pretty harmless. But after a while, when I got up to return to my own office, he would stand up and clasp me to his manly bosom. He was a tall man, of fine physique, and being rather small myself, I always found my face pressed against the brass buttons of his jacket. This was uncomfortable. It was downright unpleasant. I was the lowest rank in the WRNS and he was the highest in the establishment, responsible for the whole of the Coastal Force base. I knew he felt he was conferring some sort of honour on me. If I disillusioned him it would hurt his self-esteem, maybe irreparably. I also guessed this is what happened when Minnie kidded herself he was in love with her. I felt I couldn't say anything to either of them but began to dread being called into his office.

In the mean time we all got on pretty well together in our office. We generally had plenty of work to do but there was an occasion when one of the girls started talking about deportment and we decided to play the old game of putting a book on our heads and seeing how long we could keep it there.

"You go first, Minnie" someone said in deference to her seniority. She took only a couple of steps before it fell. Each in turn, with variable success, had a go and then I picked up a book which had been lying on my desk for some time. It was "Ariel" by André Maurois. The going had been hard because it was in French and it was taking me forever to read. (Incidentally, I still haven't finished it!). However, I did as the others had done and balanced it on my head. Almost immediately it fell off and out of it dropped a scrap of paper with writing on it. I quickly picked it up and read in French, "I hope this will amuse you. If you would like to read something very funny try Georges Courteline. Please reply on the other side if you would like to continue this correspondence." Of course, I answered, as requested.

After this we all thoroughly inspected every male who entered our office. These were mainly MTB officers but none showed any particular interest in me. Sometimes, if they were dishy, I might try to persuade myself that this was so but on the whole they were rather shy anyway. None seemed the type to have written these little notes. Yes, I mean "notes" in the plural, for they continued, mainly with recommendations of books or poetry to read, or little amusing anecdotes in French.

Day after day the first thing the girls wanted to know was whether there was another *billet-doux*. So we were all jolly disappointed when they stopped. We could almost have written a book: The Mystery of the Captain's Office. But we didn't know how to solve the mystery. Whenever the room was left empty, it was locked. If anyone came in while we were there, we now kept our eyes glued on him.

Then one day there was an order out that all Wrens who were not on duty the following evening should appear in the main hall of the Wrennery to sing sea shanties with Dame Vera Laughton-Matthews, the Director WRNS. Sea shanties? Whoever heard of Wrens singing sea shanties? Was this how she thought we spent our free time? However, we all gathered in the main hall, as requested, and this huge figure walked onto the platform followed by our Chief Officer, Mrs. Malschinger, who was a tiny lady, smaller than I am[9]. We were soon trilling away and in the middle of "What shall we do with the drunken sailor?" someone tapped me on the shoulder and whispered that a seaman was waiting in the hall to speak to me. What should I do? Would I get a bottle if I slipped out? I risked it. A huge bearded sailor awaited me.

"I'm sorry I've had to stop writing to you," he said, "but I'm going to sea."

"Tell me," I replied, "how did you get into our office?" I knew I had never seen this man before.

"Oh," he said, "I had the keys. I was your cleaner!"

I never heard from him again. Was his ship torpedoed? Did he dislike me when we met? I hope not the former. But then again, I hope not the latter.

We were always very busy in the Captain's Office and now, as well as the usual work I was asked to appear at Captain's Orders. This was a sort of mini court where less serious misdemeanours were dealt with in accordance with KR and AI (King's Regulations and Admiralty Instructions) by the Commanding Officer. I was supposed to take down the evidence but this was extremely difficult as people were inclined to mumble. I again wondered what on earth the Captain's secretary did

[9] Brenda at full height was 5 ft 2 ½ inches

all day other than entertain the Number One (the Captain's second in command) in her office, as I seemed to do all the secretarial work and more.

I say "and more" because I still hadn't dealt with the Captain's more amorous moments. However, one Sunday I was alone in the office and knew today had to be the day. I was very nervous and dreaded the moment when I knew he would ring for me. When it came, I went in, took down some letters and as he stood up, ready to embrace me, I said.

"I'd much rather you didn't do that, Sir," and got out before he could reply. I was shaking all over. Time was getting on and I decided I wasn't up to doing any more work. So I slipped round his door, opened it a little and said, "I'm going now, Sir." He jumped up, came over, laid a lordly hand on my head and said, "I've always liked you, Brenda, and always shall." It never happened again. It had all been so simple.

However, sometime after that, there was trouble with the Plumbers. Engineers in the Navy are always called "plumbers". Their offices were just across the way and their WRNS writer was upset. I was asked to replace her. They had been told that as I was the third writer they had had and would be the last if I didn't like working for them, then they would have to make do with a stoker. A new girl, Mary Quarry took over from me and I moved to the Plumbers.

I walked into their office which was in a separate small building and was confronted by a sub-lieutenant standing on his head in a battered old, velvet covered, Victorian armchair. Another sub-lieutenant stepped forward with hand outstretched, "I'm Tony," he said. "You must be Brenda." The other one restored himself to his normal way up and with very red face said, "And I'm Roy."

At that moment a lieutenant arrived. "And this is the boss," Roy added.

"Hello," Howard said, "You must be our new Wren."

He showed me a large walk-in cupboard with no door. Inside were stacks of files on the floor and a desk with a typewriter.

"This is all yours," he said. "Look, we're not awfully busy this morning. Why don't you take yourself up to the Creamery and have a cup of coffee?"

I was delighted. I could see that this was an indication they were going to make amends for whatever had happened with the previous Wrens. Like a shot I was off up Snargate Street to the Creamery. When I returned only Howard was there.

"There's another Wren upstairs in Stores. Why not make yourself known to her?"

A very large Petty Officer presided up there. Her name was Violet Highton. Anyone less like a violet I couldn't imagine.

"Whenever you're fed up," she volunteered, "come up here and we'll make you a cup of coffee."

Things were looking good, although I hadn't been that impressed with the cupboard, with no window in it, which had been allocated to me. I wondered who had forewarned them I was rather partial to a cup of coffee.

When I returned, Lieutenant Howard said, "I've left some lists of modifications and alterations for you to type, if you wouldn't mind. We're all going aboard. If anyone wants us, you don't know how long we'll be." And off they went. The work was pretty straightforward and they all seemed to lean over backwards to be civil.

After a few weeks without any warning, I suddenly heard we were to have a new Engineer Officer in charge and that Howard had been appointed elsewhere. Everyone seemed a little in awe of the new man. He had been invited to come straight into the Navy as a lieutenant commander, his qualifications were so outstanding. He appeared one morning and was introduced. He looked at my cubby hole and asked if there was anything I needed. "Yes," I told him, "a filing cabinet." This, I might add, never arrived. He was a very quiet man but tough. No more cups of coffee at The Creamery, I thought. His name was Eric Toleman[10].

I started to understand better what we were doing. He explained MTBs that had been damaged or were faulty were visited by them and a decision made as to what it was possible to do by way of repair. As you can imagine, the CO (Commanding Officer) and crew of the MTB welcomed our Engineers as the sooner the repairs were completed, the sooner they could get back to sea. They also always hoped by lavishing drink (of which they appeared to have plenty) on them, they might be persuaded to agree to items that weren't so essential but good to have. I was always being left to hold the fort whilst they went on board, I never knowing when they would return or, for that matter, in what condition.

I can still remember an afternoon when Admiralty in London kept ringing and it was with great difficulty that I staved them off. I stayed

---

[10] In the late 1950s / early 1960s Brenda and her daughter visited Eric Toleman in the Isle of Wight where, in retirement he still had some sort of boat house, Hazel remembers.

long after my normal departure time until, finally, Lieutenant Commander Toleman slunk in on his own. I gave him a thorough ticking off and he assured me he would deal with Admiralty.

"And where are the others?" I asked.

He didn't know and I left as soon as he rang Admiralty. It was a good thing he was such a brilliant engineer. He told me before the war, with a crew, he had taken yachts owned by millionaires all over the world.

Next morning the other two appeared and after a bottle from me, said they woke up in a field below the Castle as a result of having drink thrust upon them aboard each ship they visited. The inference was they hadn't wanted the booze…much!

In the meantime, Mary Quarry[11], who had taken my place in the Captain's Office, also moved into my cabin when Pat left. Doc Thompson had fallen in love with Pat, my former companion, who was a very beautiful girl, and they had decided to get married. I had been very involved in this as Doc Thompson worried greatly before proposing and kept asking me whether he should do so and whether I thought she loved him. When she accepted, they both asked me to keep it a secret. A Wren, upon marriage, could be released from the Service and after a while this is what happened.

And so it was that Mary asked me if she could take Pat's place. We got on very well together, having the same ideas about many things. Her mother lived in Tankerton, near Whitstable, which was near enough for Mary to visit her on a day off and sometimes I went with her. Another girl who had a cabin near ours was Sylvia, who was a dispatch rider. She was one of JB Priestley's daughters. I remember she was always falling off her motor bike and fracturing one limb or another. She was very attractive and always gave us a laugh.

Wendy was another girl we befriended. It was Christmas time and Mary, who was very soft-hearted, told me Wendy was hiding herself away from everybody. Couldn't we do something about her? Apparently she had been taken aboard ship by a boyfriend. Here I must explain that although I had been warned long ago to always wear pusser pants[12] when going aboard, Wendy was wearing French knickers. Do you know what

---

[11] Mary Quarry later became the wife of Desmond Scott, the naval officer and oceanographer who placed the Union Jack on Rockall and many years later directed the International Oceanographic Commission (IOC) in UNESCO.

[12] Apparently trousers.

16

these were? They were considered rather glamorous. They were made of silk or a silky material and were kept up generally by a button on the side. Well, Hazel[13], perhaps you can guess what happened. They suddenly fell down and before she could step out of them and pick them up, this gallant young man snatched them and she was later told he hung them on a line in his cabin for all to see. She felt she couldn't show her face in public after that and it took a long time to convince her that few people would be aware of the incident.

I don't know why but for some reason Wendy[14] wanted me to meet her Mother. This lady was no longer married to Wendy's Father who had been badly shell-shocked during the Great War. Her current husband was one Major Toms. We both had weekend leave in London and she rang me at home to say her Mother would like me to have dinner with them at the Mayfair Hotel.

"I'll be waiting in the foyer at 7.30," she said.

She was there, as promised, when I arrived.

"I'm afraid Mother has gone to bed," she said. "She's been helping to pack parcels at St. James's Palace. You know, for prisoners of war. She goes once a week. She said I should bring you up to her suite for coffee. Dinner's on her".

I wasn't used to eating in such style. It was quite exciting as I had never been to the Mayfair before.

We had a good old gossip over our meal. Amongst other things she told me she had been to finishing school in Switzerland. She had quite liked it but her Mother was inclined to make it difficult for her.

"For instance," she said, "I wanted to go on a trip with the school. We were all told to write to our parents for the money to pay for it. That was normally no problem. They were all daughters of parents with plenty of money. My Mother is more than a millionairess. But I couldn't go because she said she couldn't afford it. It was a long telegram, full of explanations. In fact, it cost more than I had asked for".

She had lived for several years with her grandparents and that, she said, had been a happy time. She particularly loved her grandmother.

Anyway, we finished our dinner and ventured up to see her Mother.

She was sitting up in bed, her beautiful blonde hair hanging loosely over her shoulders. On a table at her bedside stood a huge bowl of

---

[13] Hazel is Brenda's daughter for whom these memoirs were written.
[14] Wendy Sainsbury was a member of the famous grocery family.

magnificent daffodils. I suppose she was in her forties. For something to say, I admired the daffodils.

"Oh," she said, "the gardener sends me flowers every week from my house in Wimbledon."

In "Wasp" we were supposed to go down to the cellars when there was an air raid. We hated these cellars. If we could we hung back when everyone else made their way down and tried to get a night's sleep in our own beds. Our Mess was in the cellars that had acquired an unpleasant smell due to being used day and night and no fresh air penetrating. This rather put us off eating there. Mary and I had an arrangement that if one of us was invited out for a meal, we would try to make it a foursome to include the other. We were paid a pittance so we couldn't afford meals at restaurants otherwise, though we did go to the YWCA sometimes. However, the girl who was running it was inclined to serve very dainty little sandwiches which didn't fill us up. Our favourite place was the Café Royale, hardly comparable with its famous namesake in London but the best that could be found at that time in Dover. Curiously enough and despite the fact that they were the enemy, it was owned and run by Italians. Not even French, as one might have assumed by the name. The food was delicious and the place had a real feeling of Soho. There was, however, one disadvantage. The tables were placed against the walls on either side of the restaurant with a passage up the centre leading directly to the toilet, which made it pretty obvious if one had to use it. I was a bit sensitive about that.

I was surprised to learn one day that I was to be transferred to the Pens. These had recently been built, perhaps a quarter of a mile out to sea, to house the MTBs (Motor Torpedo Boats). A jetty connected them to the shore. Offices were built over the top, with an Ops Room under Lieutenant Mark Arnold-Forster[15], one of the outstanding MTB heroes of the war. This is where I was to go. Fine in itself, but it entailed moving from "Wasp" into WRNS quarters near the Pens. I was happy with the Plumbers (Engineers) but thought this might be more exciting.

I moved into my new quarters and almost immediately felt I was being frozen out. If I sat at a table in the mess, the others moved. Nobody spoke to me. However, when this antipathy stretched to our working

---

[15] Hazel finds it curious that when, like so many families we watched the TV series in 26 episodes The World at War, narrated by Olivier, Brenda never connected the accompanying book by Mark Arnold-Forster with the man under whom she had served.

environment, I was completely nonplussed. I would find my typewriter had disappeared, my chair, all sorts of things.

"I can't work if I don't have the tools," I told Mark.

"There's nothing I can do about it," he said, "We're not yet fully equipped."

His courage at sea unfortunately did not extend to matters such as this. He was desperately shy and didn't want to have to lay down the law. I, myself, had no authority as I was still the lowest rank of Wren. However, I made up my mind to find out what it was all about. As a start I discovered most of these were new Wrens who had been recently conscripted into the Service. Up to this time all Wrens had joined voluntarily and there was a feeling of comradeship amongst them. One of these new Wrens had been under the impression she was going to work in the Ops Room and resented the fact that I had been sent in her place. Instead, she was attached to the Captain's Office at "Wasp" to gain a little experience. The long and the short of it really was that none of these Wrens wanted to be in the WRNS in the first place and had no intention of trying to make a go of it. I rang Mary and asked her to meet me in town.

It had been a miserable, foggy day and in the evening we went to the flicks to cheer ourselves up with a good cry over "Mrs. Miniver". I left Mary outside the cinema as we were now going in opposite directions, she to "Wasp" and I, for the first time after dark, to my new quarters near the Pens.

The fog seemed thicker now but I knew that once on the front, it was a straight walk to the Wrennery. I started on my way, putting my handkerchief over my nose and mouth. I stepped out smartly, the quicker to get there. But very soon I became doubtful of where I was. I stood still a moment, wishing intensely that we had lighting. If I had even had a torch with me, it would have been a help. I knew I had only to take a right turning to be by the sea but I couldn't remember whether or not I had done that. I didn't know whether I was on the pavement or in the road. I stopped again and listened for the sea and thought I heard it. The other way, down Snargate Street, was always busy at this time in the evening, so Mary would easily find her way back. As long as the pubs were open, there were people about but here I didn't see or hear a soul. I think even the sound of German planes I would have welcomed as something natural that I was used to.

I stood still for a few seconds to collect my thoughts. Was I imagining

19

it or was the fog getting even thicker? I could hardly breathe with the handkerchief to my face and put it in my pocket. I asked myself if I was doing the sensible thing. Perhaps I should turn back. But I was no longer sure of my way back either, so I told myself to plough on.

In this silent world, without warning, the shock came. A loud shout and I could see the nozzle of a rifle pointed directly at me a few steps away.

"Halt! Who goes there?"

Nobody had warned me. My heart was thumping at a pace it had never thumped before. What was I supposed to answer?

"Friend!" I shouted back but only a small sound came.

"Advance friend and be recognized," came the reply.

I walked forward nervously. It had sounded a bit like play acting but even so, I was shaking like a jelly.

"I'm trying to find my way back to the Wrennery," I told him. He lowered his rifle.

"Your pass, please," he said.

I had no pass but showed him my pay book which seemed to satisfy him. To tell the truth, I think he was rather relieved I wasn't a German.

"Am I on the front?" I asked him.

"Yes. You just carry straight on for about a couple of hundred yards and you'll be at the Wrennery."

I knew there would be no welcoming friends when I arrived back, so I went straight to my bunk and considered what to do. A transfer seemed the only answer.

The next day we had a visit from Mrs. Churchill and Mrs. Roosevelt[16], who came to see the nearest point to the French coast and, of course, to the Germans. The Ops Room being the centre of action, they were very interested to see it and us. Mrs. Roosevelt had apparently been very anxious to see what was happening in Dover. She was a large, very active woman and the story goes that her energy exhausted Mrs. Churchill who at one point, being unable to keep up with her companion, just sat down on the ground! But this did not compensate for my general unhappiness

---

[16] There was an account by Jack Fishman, journalist and writer, of this visit, part of a three-week tour. "I vividly remember the things we saw at Dover," recalled Mrs. Roosevelt. "There had been a bombing at the WRNS' headquarters and we went to see what the damage had been, and also went to see the ships that they took care of. We visited the places where people took refuge in the cliffs. It was a revealing tour because I had come from America where we knew none of this. It was very enlightening."

and at the first opportunity I took myself off to Admin.

"We do need a Writer for a few weeks in Folkestone," an officer told me. "Theresa Longstaff is going on compassionate leave to-morrow. You would fill in the gap while I see where you'd be most useful."

The WRNS were very good over things of this sort, trying to fit a round peg into a square hole, which I believe was not so in either of the other women's services.

"There's no Wrennery there but there's a boarding house where we can fix you up. Theresa Amphill, the Admiral's driver - the only other Wren - lives at home."

This sounded quite interesting. No rules and regulations!

In due course I was given all the details and discovered I was to go there by car the next afternoon with Rear Admiral Round-Turner who was the NOIC (Naval Officer-in-charge) Folkestone. I can't say I was anything but pleased at this transfer but did wonder what was going on. Being so close to Dover, Folkestone did not need a large establishment and I found it a wonderful change from the enormous staff in the former. Admiral Round-Turner was a delightful old chap who had two daughters in the WRNS. He had already retired when war broke out but as Admirals never officially retire he was recalled and given the rank of Captain, although always referred to as Admiral Round-Turner.

This turned out to be a very happy few weeks. In my recollection there were only four of us working in the Harbour Master's House: the Admiral, his driver, Laura, a lieutenant (possibly two) and me. The Admiral spent some time teaching me navigation and the lieutenant instructed me on the use of the radio for sending messages. Everything was fun. On a day when he had to see Admiral Ramsey, Laura begged him "Oh, do let's take Brenda with us", his reply was, "All right, let's all go to Dover". He was always like that, full of goodwill and kindness.

At the end of this short break in Folkestone, I arrived back at "Wasp" to discover my name had been put forward for a commission[17] and I was to report to the Royal Naval College at Greenwich in a few days' time. With all the changes I had made recently I had thought the powers that be were dissatisfied with me whereas it was apparently the reverse. To say I was astonished was to put it mildly.

---

[17] Service record notes 19 Sept 1943 promoted to 3rd Officer, recommended by N. Malschinger July 1943 Wasp. 18 Sept 1943 Confirmation of promotion requested from Inverness Force S.

3. 3rd Officer Heimann prepares for the Invasion of Normandy 1943-1944

Greenwich was a wonderful experience. To sit in the Painted Hall at long refectory tables and be waited on by white gloved stewards was something I had never anticipated happening to me. It was altogether awe-inspiring. From time to time a senior officer would take a seat beside me and most people believed this was in some way part of the exercise. I felt I was doing reasonably well until it came to the squad drill. I had always disliked this nor could I see any point in it. Within a short time of arriving in Dover I discovered if one could not be spared from one's work it was possible to be excused squad drill. After that I saw to it that I could never be spared. Be sure your sins will find you out. So the saying goes and it turned out to be all too true. One of the tasks one was put through was to march a squad of Wrens round Greenwich, not just the College environs but in the streets around us. This caused me nightmares. When the dreaded day arrived I managed to get them started but kept forgetting the correct orders and not only did I nearly get them run over but only stopped them just in time to avoid marching into a wall. Only the ghastly tales of others finding themselves in similar situations gave me some relief.

In view of this awful performance I was surprised to be passed out. But I was able to order my uniform when the various tailors arrived. Lillywhites made mine. We were to be given £50 each towards the cost and, surprisingly, this did more or less cover it.

And so I emerged from the Royal Naval College an officer, with instructions to report to WRNS Headquarters in Queen Anne's Mansions, St. James's Park.

I found here that I was working with a small group of girls, supervised by a 2nd Officer WRNS, on Officers' Appointments. I longed to be back at WASP and wondered if I had made some ghastly mistake to have accepted promotion without demur. However, in my second week I was sent for by Admin.

"Captain Adams at HMS "WASP" has requested your return," I was told quite kindly, "would you like to go back there?"

I thought it a terrific compliment but felt it wouldn't work. All my friends were ratings and consorting with them rather than the officers would not be smiled upon. However much I might disapprove of this, it would be difficult.

"What kind of an appointment would you like?" I was asked at WRNS HQ.

"Something close what is happening in the war," I said, "something operational."

"Right! I could send you to Scotland. Your exact location would be secret, even to your family. They will be able to write to you to a PO Box address which will be given to you before you go."

When I returned to our office I felt quite excited. Although how Scotland could bring me nearer to the war was quite beyond me. I told the others as much as I knew and one of them, a girl named Mary Gardiner, asked me if I would mind if she asked to be sent there too.

"You see, my home's in Edinburgh."

She was the storybook kind of Scots girl, with wonderful red hair.

I went home and told my parents. I had been living at home whilst working at WRNS Headquarters as it was an easy journey to St. James's Park. My Mother was quite proud of me, I think, as she loved going out with me when I was in uniform. However, I only worked at WRNS HQ for a month before being despatched to Scotland.

Mary invited me to spend the night at her parents' home in Corstorphine Road in Edinburgh and then, on reporting as bidden, we were instructed to continue our journey as far as Inverness and were given first class rail tickets as we were now officers. I had begun to think we were on our way to Scapa Flow. However, once in Inverness, we were taken to Cameron Barracks where a Chief Officer, Betty Samuel was in charge of the WRNS. These Barracks belonged to the Cameron Highlanders. In September they were already bleak. They were full of Portacabins, which I think we called huts. Our quarters, however, were in the main building and the huts were used for offices.

Another girl, Barbara, had now joined us and the three of us awaited a male officer, a Lieutenant Matthews. We got to know some of the girls and all seemed very likeable. We worked side by side, but not together, with some of the army and enjoyed their company, one evening a week learning to dance the Scottish reels.

We were now informed we were attached to Force S[18], training to take part in the invasion of Normandy. Mary and another girl, Barbara, were to work in one room on Personnel, whilst I was to work in one next to theirs with a Lieutenant Downing, who was more or less in charge. I was called "M" standing for Materiel and I was quite horrified to be given a long list of subjects for which I was responsible and about which I reckoned I knew nothing. I recently came across this list, which I believe to be worth repeating, so here goes: Maintenance, Repair facilities, Docking, Refits, Defects, A and As, Stores - Naval, Armament, Communications, Navigation, Victualling and clothing, Fuel, Water, Ammunition, Salvage, Moorings - berths, Accommodation, Works and buildings, Organisation of Shore Establishments, Communications, Mails, Material returns, Censorship, Security, Transport, Charts, Equipment - radar, gunnery, electrical, V/H, R/T.

The procedure was that stacks of papers were delivered to me in our office. These had to be read through with the relevant documents and a minute sheet which had already been attached and if I could deal with them without help I was to write on said minute sheet what should be done. Of course, it rarely happened that I could deal with things without getting advice from experts who were responsible for that particular subject, so down the side of the minute sheet I would put the titles of those concerned asking for their comments, ending the list with "M" so it would be returned to me to deal with finally. If a letter was to be written, it was up to me to write it at the bottom of the minute sheet and send it elsewhere to be typed.

I believe this was a Civil Service system of doing things but as I had never been in the Civil Service nor even on an Admiral's staff, it was all new to me. It wouldn't have been too bad if there hadn't been such shoals of documents loaded onto my desk all day. Lieutenant Downing was also overworked and too busy to help me. Barbara frequently volunteered to come back with me in the evening and she was a great help. We naturally became very good friends.

It might be worth breaking here to tell you about her. She was the daughter of a retired surgeon and the niece of a Rear Admiral. Her father

---

[18] Assault Force 'S', was the combined army and navy force due to take part in the D-Day invasion at Sword Beach. It trained during the winter 1943-1944 in the area around Inverness.

had been recalled to the Newcastle Infirmary when they were short staffed due to the war. He had been a medical missionary in China prior to that, and Barbara's sister, who was also a doctor, worked in China as well with her doctor husband. Sadly, her husband was killed there. Barbara's own story is unbelievably sad too. She was engaged to a young man who was at that time missing presumed dead. After two years she became engaged to a boy she had known all her life, but, unfortunately, he was taken prisoner in Japan. In the meantime, she received a printed card from the first one saying he was a Japanese prisoner of war. Within two weeks of this, she was officially informed he had been shot and killed trying to escape from the camp. This was after the invasion of Normandy and she applied to WRNS HQ to be sent abroad and went to Ceylon. Sometime after, Dick, her second fiancée, escaped from his prisoner of war camp, somehow got to Europe, walked most of the way home, walked into his parents' home in Northumberland, where his mother had such a shock she suffered a heart attack and died.

It is almost unbelievable, isn't it? Dick was in a terrible state and Barbara's father didn't want them to get married until he was more stable but they didn't want to wait. They had no children and Dick died at an early age. Eventually, Barbara married a widower with quite a large family and she suddenly found happiness amongst this family, whom she genuinely adopted as her own and they too, seemed fond of her. I can't remember for how long she was married, perhaps twenty years, but she died of cancer just a few years' ago.

Anyway, to get back to Force S...As you may have gathered, it was not an easy job. We were aware that this seemingly impossible undertaking would be happening in a very few months and many men's lives were at stake. In such circumstances, it was impossible to demand too much of us and the nearer we came to D-Day, the harder we worked. After all, what was asked was nothing in comparison with that which the men were facing.

On top of that, we had a very difficult Admiral's secretary to deal with. He sent for me and told me he was going to inspect daily all my work. He had an irritating habit of tilting his chair backwards as he spoke. Captain Hallett, who worked in an office near mine, got onto the Admiral's secretary and told him I had more sense in my little finger than he would have if he lived to be a hundred. Captain Hallett was the senior of the two officers, so after that the Secretary, if he phoned Captain Hallett, always said he was speaking for the Admiral. Eventually, he had Captain Hallett moved from Cameron Barracks into the Caledonian Hotel, which proved very useful when we had no water at the Barracks. He rang me and said, "I can smell you over the telephone. Come down here and use my bathroom!"

There was a lighter side too. The Army was there, too, at Cameron Barracks and one of the chaps, Charles Wildblood, asked whether, if he arranged for a piper to come once a week, would some of the Wrens join them in learning the Scottish reels. For a long time this became a regular feature of our social life and was wonderful exercise which we all enjoyed.

By Christmas we had all settled down into our routine. New friendships were no longer new and we were all aware of what was expected of us. On Christmas morning I was invited to join a few senior Naval officers who were going to church and then back to their mess for pre-lunch drinks. It was a lovely, crisp morning. I can't for the life of me remember what happened at lunchtime but I think it most likely we served the lower deck (other ranks), which is a Naval tradition, and in the evening had our own celebrations.

Betty Samuel was an exceptional Chief Officer, known to most people as Chief "O", and very popular with both men and women. She offered open house in our ante-room for tea on Sunday afternoons and we were never short of guests. No-one ever asked another exactly what his or her work entailed as it was generally accepted that secrecy in every way was more important than anything else.

As time went by I was not the only one working in the evenings. At midnight the place was often much the same as at midday. We still tried to give ourselves time off for Highland dancing although there were occasions when someone or other had to skip the evening. Before things became too frantic a few of us visited Loch Ness and looked for the Monster! We stayed at a hotel in Drumnadrochit and fell in love with that area. Six of us, or was it four, managed to get away for a weekend to visit Loch Ness and the Monster. Barbara came and Cedric, one of Charles's friends. When time permitted Charles and I would sometimes have a meal together and on one of these occasions we bumped into an old friend of mine from peacetime London. It seemed quite extraordinary to see Ralph, in Army uniform, way up in the north of Scotland, having dinner with a girlfriend. He was a much more attractive man than Charles but the latter was better company. We did not allow things to go beyond close friendship although I was a bit in love with Charles, as I knew he was married. In those days our morals were different from those of today. Possibly the invention of the birth control pill changed this.

I dreaded D-Day arriving and maybe discovering many of our friends had been killed. No-one ever asked another about his work as it was generally accepted secrecy was more important than anything else. I knew Charles had something to do with Security and that he conducted a session in French every day. I imagined he and his men would have to try and divert the attention of the enemy away from the true manoeuvres once they reached the French coast. I admired their courage and wondered how on earth they were able to summon it.

I had been to one of the rehearsals, the Moray Firth standing in for the French coast. The men had been sitting out in their landing craft for 24 hours longer than expected due to the weather which was bitterly cold. I should think at least 50 per cent of them had been seasick but still had to jump into the drink and wade ashore with rifles and clobber. I had been told that as soon as possible after D-Day two or three of us, including me as my job would continue on the other coast, would follow the men.

As D-Day drew nearer we all moved south but it meant the break-up of our unit. I went with probably the greater number to Pompey, the Naval name for Portsmouth. Barbara and several others went to the HQ of Overlord, Fort Southwick at Fareham and maybe Mary Gardiner went there too. Charles and his group were sent to Petersfield.

This is a letter from A.D. Divine, War Correspondent to the "Daily Sketch"[19]:

When the captain of one landing craft opened his sealed orders at H-hour on receiving the invasion key-word, a typewritten slip was among the mass of instructions and information. It read:

We've been with you through northern winds
And ice and snow and rain,
We followed you south to the land of the sun
And helped you all to train;
But now the time has come for us
To say goodbye to you
We wish you luck and pray that God
Will bring you safely through.

---

[19] Cutting still amongst Brenda's papers.

It was signed "The Wrens".

No, I didn't write it but I must have delivered it, for, the day before D-day I travelled the length of the coast from Portsmouth to Dover with sealed orders for Commanding Officers of ships taking part in "Overlord", the invasion of Normandy.

With D-day drawing nearer, we had all moved south but it meant the break-up of our unit, Force-S. I went to Pompey, Barbara to the headquarters of "Overlord" and Charles and his group to Petersfield.

"We're so full up here," one of the Admin types told us, "we didn't know where to put you but we've given you an empty school. In the circumstances, I hope you'll be all right."

It was true, of course. The Port was overflowing with men and women from all the Services and more were arriving hourly. Many were camped under the trees.

The first night there was an air raid warning. There was a shelter just outside into which we shepherded all the girls.

One of the other officers said to me,

"Do let's slip back inside when they're all settled."

So three of us saw the rest into the shelter but decided ourselves to remain more comfortably in our ante-room. It was unlikely after all we would get a direct hit. How wrong we were!

The bombers started flying over and we rammed our tin hats on our heads, lay down on the floor and wished we were in the shelter with the others. Then one bomb seemed too close for comfort. One of us remembered someone had left a little dog in her room as animals were not allowed in air raid shelters. She dashed in, picked it up and came back with the news that the outside wall at the back of the building had collapsed. As soon as there was a lull, we slipped into the shelter, dog and all, and stayed there till the "All clear" went.

After this episode, we were moved out of the school. The powers that be decided after all we could share accommodation with Wrens not attached to Force S. The Admiral said as soon as the invasion started the Wrens were to be given a rest. I longed for it but dreaded it. Our many friends were at last obliged to face this ordeal and who knew how many would come through it. I had seen an exercise in the Moray Firth in Scotland when the waves were so high the men were terribly seasick. In this state they had had to jump from the landing craft into the freezing sea, with their ammunition, and wade ashore. That was bad enough but this would be the real thing.

I had only seen Charles and the other boys a couple of times since our arrival in Pompey but on the eve of the landings they asked two or three of us to come out to their barracks at Petersfield to say goodbye. I had a deep dread inside me of what the morning might bring and they, surely, must have wondered whether they would live to tell the tale...

Others not far away, set sail from the Isle of Wight during that night and bombers had attacked the concrete fortifications along the Normandy coast. By dawn there was great activity in Pompey. Our own work being temporarily in suspension, we watched from a room overlooking the sea as the landing craft set out towards Arromanches on the French coast. From then on our information came by radio as the whole country was kept informed about what was happening. We watched and listened all day. There was no doubt about it that the Germans had been taken by surprise and casualties were far fewer than expected at Arromanches but we had no news of individuals.

We had all worked for about eight months preparing for this day and now it had come. We, the Wrens, with a WAAF Officer, Camilla, waved the men goodbye from windows overlooking the harbour, although, of course, they were unaware of us. We had the radio on following every word uttered and our hearts were in our mouths. I felt we should be ahead of the broadcast news but we were not, we heard exactly the same as everyone else in the country who wanted to listen, television not as yet being available.

Later that day I was informed that three of us, that is two men and me, had to take it in turns to go on duty all night in case there were any calls from the landing beaches. I still had gyppy tummy but it seemed so unimportant compared with what was happening that I still did not report it. But it dragged me down and I was now overcome by tiredness. My nights on duty were spent alone on the fourth floor of the building, the room containing a bed and a telephone. I had little sleep as I was afraid of missing a call from the French coast but, anyway, the bombers flying over kept me awake. In the morning I returned to the Wrennery, had a bath and breakfast and was on duty again in the office. Mind you, I wanted to be there as I was desperate for news of how things were progressing. Fortunately, the landings at Arromanches, our section, had gone better even than expected. It was almost too good to be true. Not so for the Americans. Their men were immediately confronted by a German contingent carrying out an exercise to withstand just such an attack as this. Their losses were heavy. As far as I could find out none of my friends had been killed thank goodness. Our people were pressing on into France and I was later shown a picture of Charles shaking hands with a Frenchman, possibly the Mayor of Caen, with a caption underneath saying he was the first British Army officer to enter Caen.

After a while we no longer needed a Duty Officer at night as everything was going well. Other than a request to send over a crane which was needed urgently, I can't remember any calls. Despite this I felt too exhausted to carry on in the day and I told the Lieutenant I was taking a day's leave to go up to London to WRNS HQ. He didn't like it. He, too, was just as tired as I was. At WRNS HQ I told them I still wanted to follow the men to France when the time came but that I was worn out through lack of sleep. They told me to take some leave and let them have the address where I would be. When I returned to Pompey, I found a note from Lieutenant Matthews saying he had taken a day's leave to visit Admiralty. After a few days I packed my things and said goodbye to Pompey. Usually my Father came to Victoria to meet me. This time, however, it was Bunny who was there to tell me Daddy had been in a Lyons Teashop in Kensington High Street which had had a direct hit. Thank goodness, he was one of the more fortunate people as about seventeen had been killed. However, he had lost a finger and was in the West London Hospital. We went straight there and were glad to find him reasonably well under the circumstances and were assured by the staff there was nothing to worry about. They said everyone fit to travel was being transferred to Bourne End Hospital in Buckinghamshire. My Mother decided to find digs there so that she could visit him every day.

Once my Mother had gone, there seemed no point in staying in an empty house, sleeping on the kitchen floor every night. I rang Auntie May in Cheshire and asked if I could spend a week or two with her. I liked my cousins, Julie and Mabel, and quite looked forward to seeing them all.

Barbara, who happened to be in London, saw me off at Euston, and I told her I was getting dreadful pains in the tummy. I tried to hide these from my Aunt and Uncle but it was impossible. They insisted I went to their doctor which I felt obliged to do. He dispensed his own medicines and gave me a bottle of some clear, pink stuff which I dutifully took but was no better. Next time he gave me cloudy pink stuff which had the same negative result. Then, of all things, my papers arrived to go to Normandy. Amongst them was a list of what are called Admiralty Surgeons and Agents and instructions to go to one of them to get inoculations etc. before departing. I promptly 'phoned the nearest and he came over to see me. He immediately said I had gastro-enteritis and was in no fit state to have these injections. I rang WRNS HQ who said they were sorry and would I let them know as soon as I was better. I was very distressed but decided I would be well in about a week. However, this doctor could not be persuaded I must have the inoculations and weeks went by when I was quite sure I was well enough to go. He had known his job inasmuch as all symptoms had disappeared and I was now up and about.

I was getting anxious that I might miss this so I rang WRNS HQ and told them I was now well and ready for France. "Sorry," was the reply, "we couldn't wait for you. We had to send someone else. We do need one Wren in Paris, but after your recent illness we don't think it suitable for you - the hygiene isn't too good." If I couldn't go to Normandy, the prospect of being the only Wren in Paris certainly had its attractions.

But they couldn't be persuaded. "Stay at home for the time being. We shall be in touch soon." As good as her word, she rang me again. "How would you like to go to Italy?" she enquired. In the circumstances I considered this a very impressive appointment. "I'd love to," I said. I hung up the 'phone and danced round the hall. Truly, I had thought I was designated for some dull administrative job, like my first on leaving Greenwich.

Brenda 2nd row extreme right - Greenwich

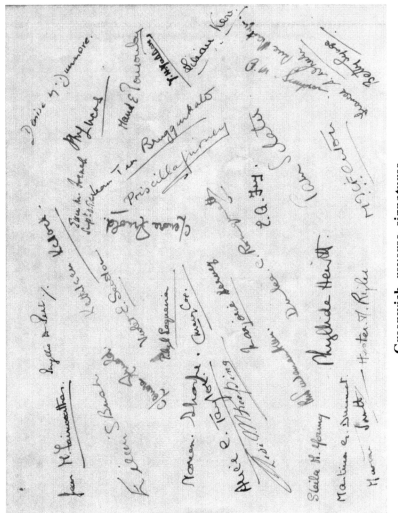

Greenwich, reverse, signatures

Barbara Stevens, Inverness

Inverness

Mary Gardiner, Inverness

Wrens' Wish

From A. D. DIVINE,
'Daily Sketch' War Correspondent

WHEN the captain of one landing craft opened his sealed orders at H-hour on receiving the invasion key-word, a typewritten slip was among the mass of instructions and information. It read:

" We've been with you through northern winds and ice and snow and rain.

" We followed you south to the land of the sun and helped you all to train,

" But now the time has come for us to say ' Goodbye' to you.

" We wish you luck and pray that God will bring you safely through! "

It was signed " The Wrens."

Wrens' wish

4. Italy 1945[20]

So - my papers came, instructing me to report to Crosbie Hall, a beautiful house on the Chelsea Embankment. Everyone there was going abroad somewhere and while we awaited embarkation we attended lectures, were kitted out with tropical clothes (in my case I was told I would need both, normal uniform and tropical) and generally prepared for our new adventure. I made friends with a 2nd Officer named Audrey who, like me, was setting sail for Naples.

Audrey was an only child and her background was very different from mine. She and her parents lived in the centre of London, in a huge flat in Earls Court Square. She had been presented at Court, a "must" in those days for a girl from the top crust of society. She had a decided talent for painting, in which she took after her mother who was a sculptor and very good artist. Her mother was the greatest influence in her life. Audrey was a very gentle girl but also very determined.

One other girl joined us when we went aboard the "Arundel Castle" and her name was Michal. I was two or three years older than Audrey and Michal was probably seven or eight years older than I was. She was very worldly-wise. We gathered she was a writer - not in naval sense of the word but in civilian terms. By comparison, Audrey and I were very immature.

In peacetime, all the Castle ships ploughed backwards and forwards between England and South Africa which gave me the opportunity to write to my Father that I could imagine him doing just that in this ship. We had not been allowed to give anyone the name of our vessel and so I hoped this might give him a hint. Of course, I later discovered it hadn't done any such thing.

It was September 1944. We sailed in convoy and it was an amazing sight to be surrounded by other ships as we wended our way towards Italy. It took about ten days and was very enjoyable except for the Bay of Biscay. As members of the Women's Royal Naval Service I felt we could not possibly be seasick. It would be letting the side down. It took two days at least and it was with the utmost difficulty I managed to avoid

---

[20] Service record indicates that Brenda was assigned to Station Mediterranean from 28 March 1945 until 20 September 1945.

throwing up. Audrey, too, felt ghastly. Michal we didn't even see. She told us she had been appointed Assistant Staff Officer (Intelligence) in Malta. In 1941 and 1942 Malta had suffered terribly from German bombing doubtless due to the fact that it was the Headquarters of the British Royal Navy in the Mediterranean. Since the War this HQ had had to move several times, although all the Services had forces there. I wanted very much to see this important Island.

For something to do, some of the Army on board had decided to put on a play and broadcast it to all aboard. They asked for volunteer actors and so I went along. They were doing "Parnell" and I was chosen for the part of Katie O'Shea. This surprised me as I was not good at brogues and this, without doubt, required an Irish one. However, George, the chap who was organising it, the producer I suppose I should say, told me not to worry too much about that so long as I read the part with sincerity. Yes, I did say "read" because there was neither the time nor the necessity to learn it. That is the joy of broadcasting. We did, of course, have one or two rehearsals and the final product went down very well. We received plenty of congratulations and I enjoyed the whole thing.

We reached Malta after about nine days. It looked lovely in the sunset but unfortunately only people whose final destination it was were allowed ashore. A big disappointment. However, we wished Michal good luck and sailed on to Naples.

After reporting our arrival, we were sent to the Wrennery, a rather elegant house in a side street, the Via Chiaia, where nowadays I understand the famous couture fashion houses are established. Next morning we were to be picked up and taken to Caserta where we would be working in the Palace (AFHQ) and quartered in a school nearby. Audrey and I had become good friends by this time and I was very glad of her company. It was a bit of a disappointment not to be staying in Naples but were told we could use the Wrennery, just off the Via Roma, any time we wanted to spend the night there. The journey to Caserta took about an hour - about 20 miles inland. Many of the streets in Naples were hung with huge banners announcing them to be VD areas, and it was forbidden even to stop in some of the villages through which we drove. At this time, September 1944, the Italians had capitulated in the south of the country but there was still fighting in the north of Italy.

When the Palace of Caserta was built - finally completed in 1774 - it was meant to rival that of Versailles. I believe it is, in fact, bigger but certainly not better. However, it is a very imposing building and had become the Allied Forces Headquarters, known as AFHQ. Admiral Sir John Cunningham was Commander-in-Chief of the Mediterranean, known as C-in-C Med.

Michal turned out not to be the only one to work for Naval Intelligence as I, too, found myself on the staff of S.O.I. (Staff Officer Intelligence). There was one other WRNS Officer in the section, a very glamorous, dark haired beauty named Bobbine. She always arrived very early in the morning, generally well before 8 o'clock, to sort through the signals that had arrived during the night. This gave her time later in the morning to paint her nails (not allowed in the WRNS), fix her hair (which she managed with great dexterity) and generally take care of her appearance. She didn't seem to mind how early she got up in the morning, however late she had retired to bed the previous night, as I often found her ironing her clothes at about 6 o'clock when I was staggering along to the showers more dead than alive.

Our office was a magnificent room on the first floor with a huge stone balcony overlooking the grounds, through which ran an ornamental stream from just below us to the far end where it changed its character and became a tumbling cascade washing over the stone figures of statuary. Many rooms in the Palace had been subdivided by partitions to make two or three offices and, large as it was, ours was one of these. It took me a while to be able even to find my way to this office. In one of the adjoining rooms I frequently passed an Italian cleaner washing the floors and singing in the most raucous voice a song in praise of the beloved leader, Mussolini. I am sure she was quite unaware that he was not also our favourite leader. Frequently, several cleaners would gather round my desk in the early morning asking "Guerra finito?" Is the war over?

I have to say here the job was a terrible disappointment to me after the responsible work I had been doing. It was "back to the typewriter" with a vengeance. I could only assume everything was so Top Secret as to require someone responsible to carry it out. For this reason I didn't complain to our Superintendent WRNS.

Audrey was attached to the Torpedo Section and seemed to like it. We shared a cabin and continued to get on very well together. We often walked by the stream and cascades which ran in a straight line through the formal gardens of the Palace, at the sides of which tiny lizards dashed in and out of the sunshine. The water appeared to come from fountains which splashed over-elaborate statuary at the far end of the grounds behind Briano, a hill from the top of which there was a magnificent view of the Italian countryside.

At about this time I received a letter from my ex-boss, Mr. Macey, at Industrial Engineering, saying George Townsend, their architect, was stationed with the Army at Capua which he believed wasn't far from Caserta and perhaps I would feel like getting in touch with him. Indeed, Capua was only about five miles away, so I contacted him and invited him to have a meal with me in our mess.

"I have the use of a jeep," he said. "Could you get the afternoon off and come for a drive?" This sounded very pleasant and I agreed immediately as it was a Sunday. He rang back a bit later and asked if he could bring another chap along who was new to the unit. I quickly invited Audrey to make up a foursome. Although it was Sunday, she couldn't get away in the afternoon but joined us for dinner in the evening. While George was stationed at Capua we had several such meetings but then he moved farther north. Audrey and Dennis Robinson, however, continued to see each other whenever possible and it didn't take me long to realise they were in love. She no longer had any interest in our social life and I had to find someone else to make up foursomes.

When George, our "Parnell" producer on board ship, rang I invited Hilda Jones to come along. She was very good company and seemed to enjoy herself. George was stationed right in Naples but collected us with another fellow and took us to a club for a meal. He seemed a nice man, was very interested in literature and poetry, in particular he loved "A Shropshire Lad" by A.E. Housman. He was sharing a flat with the other chap and after a while invited us there for a meal cooked. While we were having drinks before dinner, I became aware of music emanating from another room. That sounds nice, I thought. I have always been a sucker for those old Italian songs. I wondered where he had bought the recordings and made up my mind to ask him to get some for me. However, after drinks he opened some folding doors into the dining room and there stood a group of three musicians, a violinist, an accordion player and a mandolin player. I found this absolutely delightful but worrying also. I didn't feel a bit romantic where George was concerned but thought he was trying to tell me something through these three musicians and the elaborate meal he had arranged for us. I there and then decided to bring our friendship to an end which I did by gradually refusing his invitations.

After two or three months there was a reorganization of our department. Bobbine was moved to the next office, taking over from John Redgrave as secretary to Captain Bousfield, who was in charge of Intelligence Personnel, dealing with Appointments and I took over her job, pointing out to SO(1) that a Wren rating could do mine. This of course meant that I was not promoted to 2nd Officer rank as I was anyway senior to the WRNS rating who took over the typing job. Whilst I didn't care about rank it was foolish as I could have done with the extra money. However, I was happy with the new arrangement. Bobbine only accepted personal invitations from high ranking officers and being an exceptionally good looking, dark haired beauty there seemed to be plenty of these. I am not sure whether the fact that she was already married helped or hindered the situation. She had left her husband in Gibralter and seldom talked about him. On the other hand, she was easy enough to get on with. Whatever she had been doing the evening before she was always up early in the morning and in the office by 8am.

If we were extra busy, or if Audrey was, we would return in the evening to the almost deserted palace which was rather eerie to work in. I remember one night in particular when I suddenly heard a sort of scuffling sound behind me. I turned just in time to see a large rat running down my side of the partition. As I leaped to my feet it ran between them right over to the other side of the room. To say I was petrified would be putting it mildly. As fast as I could, I gathered up the work I was doing and rushed up to the floor above where Audrey was working and finished what I was doing there. Next day I was advised to report this unwanted presence to the Army and two men arrived with a cage. As I didn't want it near me, they put it in Captain Bousfield's office with instructions to let them know when it had an occupant. A day or two later when I arrived in the morning, a gaggle of Italian cleaners rushed to tell me the cage now had a tenant. "Come, come and see," they said to me in Italian. I resisted their attempts to get me in there. I didn't know much Italian but I knew how to say NO. After phoning the Army to come and collect their invited guest, I went out of the office, only to find on returning that Gerald Fitzgerald, one of our staff, had placed the cage, with its occupant, on my desk. "I shall not return to this office until that has been removed," I told them and departed with, I hope, dignity. When it was reported to me that it had gone, I did go back, only to discover it, in its cage, on the parapet running round the balcony, in full view of my desk.

The beautiful islands of Capri and Ischia lie off the Neapolitan coastline. The former was allocated to the Americans and the latter to us. We could visit Capri but not stay there and Capt. Byron, who had the room next to ours, organised a day's cruise for a few of us to Capri. The Island was absolutely dazzling and we climbed to Anacapri, where Axel Munthe wrote his book which drew so many people there. Vivid bougainvillea draped the walls of minuscule houses on the way. I had not realized it grew in more colours than purple: but some were orange, others red and there were oleanders growing beside them. Capri is all rock at different levels, with astounding views across the sea to the mainland in the distance. It was part of the expedition to see the Villa Rosa, and having been shown around, we sat down outside on a bench in the shade. Despite the rock, vines and olive trees flourished. We looked across to Ischia and decided the next time we had a weekend leave we would go there. As a matter of fact, Munthe's son was on our staff and he once said to me, "If you ever go to Capri tell Rosa's daughter, who is now in charge of the Villa, that you are a friend of mine and you want to see the whole of the house. Generally, she only shows visitors two rooms." "Have you been yourself since you came to Naples?" I asked him. "Oh no," was his reply, "it's far too commercialised!" That that was due to his father's book didn't seem to have struck him.

Ischia was different, a quieter island, not flamboyant like Capri. I loved it from the first glimpse I had of it. Ischia had a quiet charm all of its own. It is sometimes called "Isola Verde" and lives up to this name, much greener than Capri, not so brittle, an altogether gentler island. At least it was in 1945. Many years later, William Walton, the composer, set up home there in a house with a wonderful garden. Ischia is a bigger island than Capri and had been known for its healing baths. Monte Epomeo rises some way behind the Port, or it appears to do from many different vantage points. At that time there were very few hotels functioning but we were recommended to stay in Casamicciola. Sitting out on the terrace after a walk we watched the fishermen in their little boats, called lampare, with a light fixed to the bow to attract the fish. With the fireflies circling around, it was all very peaceful, a million miles away from the war, which, after all, was the reason we were there.

It was here we got to know Ann and later she asked Audrey and me to be bridesmaids at her wedding. She was the only WRNS Officer working at Porto d'Ischia and she had met Claude, her future husband, when his

MTB was in for a refit. The ceremony took place at the English church in Naples and then Audrey and I were taken by motor boat to Ischia for the reception. The rest of the guests went by ferry which, if I remember correctly, took at least a couple of hours, whereas we arrived in about forty minutes. Being ahead of the others, we were entertained by the NOIC (Naval Officer in Charge) in his pretty villa where he opened a bottle of champagne and we all drank their health and later transferred to the local hotel for the reception, after which we all waved Ann Gaylor and Claude Holloway goodbye as they sailed off to Positano for their honeymoon. Barbara Cartland would have delighted in it...! The NOIC invited Audrey and me to cruise around in his yacht "Wings" for the rest of the afternoon. This he had appropriated as her millionaire owner had abandoned her when the war appeared to be getting too close.

I realise looking back that I became light hearted once again when I arrived in Italy. The months working on Overlord, the invasion of Normandy, had been very hard and, much as I wanted to follow the men to France, this appointment to the Commander-in-Chief. Mediterranean, C-in-C Med's staff was giving me a chance to recover.

You might think from all this that our life in Italy was one long holiday. True, we did take advantage of every opportunity to see something of this lovely country but we also worked pretty hard. Patrick Barrow-Green, the SO(1), Staff Officer Intelligence, and I liked each other. It was hard to guess his age - possibly 35-ish. He was a bachelor, a very quiet man, turned in on himself, I would say. He was respected in his job but didn't know how to delegate work - hence his staff was generally dissatisfied. He had been a submariner, RN (as opposed to RNR or RNVR), in other words he was in the regular navy, but after a bad injury to one of his legs, he was considered unfit to be appointed to submarines. It was his great regret. For me, I could think of nothing worse than spending one's life aboard a submarine. The very idea of being shut up at the bottom of the sea to this day gives me the shivers.

I never quite understood Bobbine's standing when she was his PA. He once told me the office had been much happier since I replaced her. I always felt myself to be a dull substitute for that gorgeous, glamorous girl. Perhaps she made him feel small fry, too. She certainly chose high ranking officers as her escorts, although he himself was a commander - no mean rank.

Talking of high ranking officers, one day I received a formal invitation from C-in-C, Admiral Cunningham, to spend a weekend at his house the Villa Emma, in Posillipo. I discovered to my relief Audrey, too, had received a similar letter. It was a bit like being invited to Buckingham Palace: one couldn't refuse, so I sent a carefully worded reply in the third person, accepting. Not that I would have wanted to refuse. After all, how often in life does one get an invitation from a person of such eminence.

Nearer the time, we were told by the Admiral's Flag Officer to await the Admiral by a certain door outside the Palace on the appointed day as we would be travelling with him in his Rolls. Normally, it took an hour to reach Naples by road from Caserta. "What on earth shall we talk about?" I asked Audrey. After all we had never met the guy - in fact he was more like God to us. Mind you, his Flag Lieutenant was quite a dish but in the event he sat in front next to the driver.

The Admiral looked at his watch as soon as we went aboard. "Let's see if we can break the record," he said. So we were immediately immersed in a game. Mind you, it wasn't really a very fair game as we were preceded by two "snowdrops", two chaps on motorbikes, wearing white helmets, whose job it was to clear the road ahead of us: all vehicles and pedestrians were waved imperiously to the side until we had passed. Well, how important can you get? I mentally pinched myself to make quite sure this wasn't a dream.

But the dream was really the house itself. The Villa Emma was reputed to have been the home of Emma Hamilton, Nelson's beloved and Hamilton's wife. We were all reading a marvelous book about her, called "Miledi" by Bradda Field. When we arrived the Flag Officer whispered that he was sure we were dying to spend a penny, so he would get someone to show us to our rooms which were in the nursery suite. These two bedrooms, each with its own bathroom, were absolutely charming. The prettiest tiling had been used on the floor of the bathrooms and this ran up the sides of the baths, the walls and ceilings. The Italian owners of the Villa Emma[21] had moved into the chauffeur's quarters over the

---

[21] Part of a personal letter hand written by Brenda on WRNS headed notepaper provides a contemporary description of the weekend at the Villa Emma:
We set out from Caserta at 12.30 on Saturday. We both sat at the back of the car (Rolls of course!) with Admiral Cunningham and were preceded by two outriders. At this time of the day the roads are always crowded both with traffic and in Naples itself, with pedestrians but our outriders with an imperious gesture simply waved everything and everyone to the side of the road whilst we drove through in state. We did once to my concern nearly run an Italian over but C-in-C's only comment was a pity we did not

garages, and, we were assured, were glad to do so as they knew their house would be well cared for with Admiral Cunningham in residence. When all's said and done, the Italians were Hitler's allies, no peace treaty had yet been signed and there was still fighting in the north. We learned very little Italian because we didn't mix socially with Italians. We liked the girls who waited at table in the mess and we soon learned how to ask them for various things. But that was about the sum of it. Oh yes, I did have a couple of dresses made because socially we didn't have to wear uniform. There was great hilarity at the dressmakers as all the family congregated around me when I was having a fitting. "Troppo longo" I would say or other comment, at which the whole family would burst out laughing. Although we knew they were the enemy, I don't think they did.

To get back to the Villa Emma, I was absolutely overawed by its charm. Each room had a tiled floor through the centre of which ran patterns of flowers and this was carried throughout the house, the size of the tiles only changing according to the dimensions of each room. A huge dining room had windows covering two walls and the large round table easily

---

as it would have been one less wop to feed! This is his, and the average opinion here incidentally. Another comment he made during the weekend was that the average Tommy was far too sentimental. "You can see them for yourself," he said, "patting the heads of the wop children - I'd pat them with a sledge hammer!" I feel fundamentally he is right and yet don't like to hear it. After all they are ignorant and they are children - certainly treat the older ones, the adults and therefore responsible people, with some ruthlessness, but the thousands of Neapolitan children who throng the streets are too young to be responsible, and are already suffering for the sins of their parents in malnutrition, which is terribly apparent everywhere.

7.3.45 On arrival at the Villa C-in-C took us himself to our rooms - a small suite which he calls the Nursery. This consists of two charming bedrooms, each with its own bathroom. My bedroom was about twice the size of my own at home and looked out on the front of the house; the bathroom quite took my heart: the floor and lower half of the walls were tiled in a design of pink carnations on a white ground, rather like this: (hand drawn diagram). Badly drawn but perhaps you see what I mean - plain white tiles alternating with the patterned ones. The top half of the walls and ceiling were white and the fitted dressing table painted white also - quite unpretentious but very charming. This room looked out sideways across the sea.

One other WRNS Officer came to lunch - daughter of the King's ADC or something - Lavinia Lascelles and with Flags that completed our party.

The library, which they use entirely to sit in, has an enormous balcony running the full width of the house and looking right over the sea, with an almost sheer drop of some hundreds of feet.

The dining room is the most lovely place. Walking into it from the library the first noticeable thing is the smallness of the round table in the centre, the immensity of the windows which take up about three quarters of the space on two walls and give the most wonderful view straight over the...

seating twelve people looked tiny in the middle of the room. Here I was put next to a Captain Finnigan, who told me he was in charge of dentistry for the whole of the Med! He advised me not to do as the senior officers did, that is, demand to be treated by him. "My chap, Sylvester, at Caserta is a wizard," he said, "Go to him when you need a dentist." I might just add here that I did this not long after and he made me very nervous. He came in wearing dark glasses which seemed odd for a dentist. He excused himself immediately by explaining he had had rather a lot to drink the previous evening and had one hell of a headache. My anxiety became even more pronounced when he started drilling, still with his sunglasses on. But, scared as I was, I have to admit he didn't hurt me. Nor when I went back to him the following week and he was suffering from yet another hangover. But to get back to Captain Finnigan. In the course of conversation I told him the only other Finnigan I had ever met went to our school and was a friend of my eldest sister. "Which school did you go to?" he asked me. "La Sagesse Convent," I said. "And what was her Christian name?" "Frances," I replied, "but we called her Frankie, Frankie Finnigan." "She is my sister," he said. Isn't that amazing? Here we were, thousands of miles from home, and we discovered we had his sister in common. Not only that but La Sagesse was in Golders Green, in London, and they lived in Scotland, in Dundee if I remember rightly.

She was a boarder at our school, of course. I can't think why her parents sent her to school such a long way away.

Well, as you can imagine, that made conversation much easier. When you are suddenly confronted by a whole lot of high ranking officers, it is sometimes difficult to keep up a conversation with them.

Altogether it was rather an enchanted weekend. A great deal of the time the Admiral was working but we took ourselves off for walks. It was lovely country just round there and the Villa itself, standing high on the cliff, had wonderful views over the sea. Altogether, a never to be forgotten visit.

It had been easy to get a lift as far as Rome, the difficulty was having no guidance as to when my boss - Staff Officer Intelligence - SO(1) could spare me. I finally decided that once Audrey felt she could get away from Torpedoes for a whole weekend, I would try just telling SO(1) that I was going with her to Rome. This he accepted and Audrey organized a car to drop us there.

I spent two or three weekends in Rome. There was a hotel, I can't remember what it was called, where the Wrens were advised to stay. They could only give us a room on the top floor the first time I went and this room still contained the personal possessions of a Nazi army officer. It was as though he left in such a hurry that he couldn't take them with him. I didn't feel sorry for him. Rather the serve him right feeling overcame me - a glad feeling, too, that our soldiers had pushed him and his pals out of Rome. But it was odd for all that: all sorts of photos with inscriptions stood around. I don't know why it hadn't been cleared out before anyone else used it. I felt he had only gone a few hours before we arrived. It was not actually from choice that I spent weekends only there but I now think it the best way to see such a lovely city. Seven days all at once would have been too tiring but seeing just a few places at a time made it a more interesting experience. I much preferred it to Paris and wished the two cities were situated the other way round, so that it would be easy to pop across the Channel and visit it whenever I felt so inclined.

We couldn't wait to get out and just wander around Rome. These days many people spend their holidays abroad but not then. My Father had always encouraged us to save up until we had enough money to venture a little farther but I had never been as far as the South of Italy before. On this our first day we breathed in the Roman air and wandered around admiring everything from the beautiful silk dresses to the Colosseum. It was too late in the day to visit any of the famous buildings but we flung our arms wide open full of the sheer joy of being in Italy. It was another life in Italy. How I loved it! We didn't really have much time for holiday pursuits but after Normandy the whole thing seemed very like one long holiday.

On my first visit of course I had to see St. Peter's. Standing in the Piazza San Pietro, I had to tell myself this was really me. What was I doing here? I stood in awe and tried to recollect what my Father had told me about it. All I could really remember was that everyone kissed the toe of the statue of St. Peter and that my Grandmother had refused to do this in case she picked up germs from all the other hundreds of people kissing it! So I walked inside the Cathedral and had a look at the toe she wouldn't kiss. I decided to follow her example and also refrained from this act. I wondered what she would have thought had she known that next time I had an audience with the Pope - albeit with a number of other people. He wasn't a man to be admired but I wasn't aware of that till later.

On that first visit I also had to see the Piazza di Spagna where Keats lived for a time and where he died, and the Colosseum and to imagine all those poor Christians who were fed to the lions.

Sometime later I was entitled to seven days' leave and had been cogitating about where to go. It was this girl, Freda Bonnen, who made me do it. I suppose after what she'd been through, anything else seemed child's play. I didn't even know her as those who worked watches tended to pal up with others doing the same, otherwise one's free time never really matched up properly.

Anyway, they were cypher officers and had mainly been brought up to be ladies, you know, presented at court and all that. Audrey would have fitted in well as a cypher officer. We secretarial types were rather middle class, had learned shorthand and typing, and some of us had even worked before joining the WRNS. But I suppose they were a pretty nice bunch on the whole.

For all that, it surprised me when someone said one of these cypher types named Freda wanted to know who I was. She sorted me out a few days' later and told me she was due for seven days' leave and someone had told her I was, too. Would I consider hitching to Yugoslavia with her? Was she mad, I asked. It would create an international incident if we were discovered in Yugoslavia. She knew I worked for SO(1). That stood for Staff Officer (Intelligence), so she probably thought I was over cautious. She was silent for a few minutes. "I've thought it out quite carefully," she said, "and have the promise of an air hitch from an RAF type." But I think she could see I wouldn't play ball. "How about Venice, then?" she enquired tentatively. This, too, seemed rashness itself to me for everyone knew Wrens weren't allowed north of Rome. After all, there was still fighting in northern Italy. Well, you can see my dilemma. After what I'd heard about her being shipwrecked leaving Singapore and spending days in the drink in a Carley float, I could hardly crib at going to Venice. "Could we also go to Florence?" I asked. That sealed it; we were on.

It wasn't difficult to get transport to Rome. There were always people going backwards and forwards from Caserta and as soon as I let it be known that we had to get there, it was arranged. But I could hardly tell anyone we were going to Venice. Not that the men would have cared but if our WRNS Superintendent had got to hear of it, there would have been a shindy. She couldn't help it, poor thing, after all she was supposed to be responsible for us. When I look back on those days, I think she must have been rather a sport. Anyway, she was always nice to me.

Freda didn't worry about anything. I think she was pleased I arranged the trip from Caserta to Rome but she could just as easily have done it herself. From there we just hitched lifts. During the war it wasn't like today. Now I wouldn't dream of hitching a lift anywhere. But then we felt as safe as anyone could be. Then people tried to help each other. There was a terrific feeling of comradeship. As a matter of fact, the first large army staff car that came by stopped. Its only occupant was the driver and he said he could take us part of the way. He was a nice man and wouldn't leave us until he found someone else to take us on.

It was a boiling hot day in May. If you can imagine it being about a hundred times hotter than the hottest day in England and if you can imagine four of us, two large Australians and us, squashed up in the front of a huge army truck in all that heat, you can get some idea of what it was like. But they were good fun, those two chaps, and so courteous. They treated us like princesses but we felt like nursing sisters. But no, that's not quite true, we only looked like them in our white tropical uniforms. When the boys kept calling us "Sister", we thought it better than it getting around that there were a couple of Wrens in the convoy. Oh yes, I nearly forgot to mention that we were in a huge convoy of army trucks, hundreds of them just like the one in which we were. Every now and then they all stopped if the country was wooded and how I envied them! Hundreds of men would jump down and disappear amongst the trees. I didn't dare nor did Freda most of the time. It was very awkward just two women and hundreds of men. But after several hours, Freda took her courage in both hands and jumped out when the men did and managed to spend her penny without any embarrassment at all. But I was always the worrier and I just couldn't bring myself to follow suit. It became a terrible anxiety and that's probably what started me worrying about other things, too. Just supposing, I thought, there should be an accident on the road. I knew exactly what would happen. As, by this time, just about everyone in the convoy knew there were a couple of nursing sisters with them, someone would come rushing for us to attend the wounded. I couldn't stand the sight of blood and I wondered how Freda would manage. She had told me a little about what had happened when she was shipwrecked. She said one man, a doctor, spent his time swimming around from one lifeboat to another, doing what he could for everybody. Poor chap, he was drowned before rescue came. She admired him so much, she decided there and then when the war was over she would study like mad and become a doctor herself. Just fancy, at a time like that, making such a decision. I couldn't ask her in front of our two Australian boys but I hoped she had managed to find out a bit about medicine already but I doubted it.

I don't know how many hours we spent on the road but at last they told us they would have to leave us in Siena. They would take us to the YWCA there and try to find someone to take us on to Venice. It was early evening and we were desperately tired, so we were happy at the thought of a good sleep. Siena was full of one way streets. They wanted to put us down right outside the YW but every time we reached one end of the road or the other, we were faced with a NO ENTRY sign. In the end they parked nearby and humped our baggage to the front door. They really were nice chaps. They even came back later with a buddy of theirs who promised to pick us up next morning and take us to Venice. You certainly did meet some kind people in those days. And now I come to think of it, we never were called upon to attend the sick and dying.

We felt much better after a night's sleep. We were ready and waiting when Joe picked us up next morning. We saw just a little of Siena as we drove out of the beautiful city: the Piazza del Campo and the Torre del Mangia, over three hundred feet high and built in the 14th century.

We really felt we were nearing the fighting zone when we crossed the River Po over a Bailey bridge and saw all the wreckage around the old city of Bologna.

Of course, the truck couldn't go into Venice as even in wartime nothing could be done about all those canals and narrow pedestrian streets. "Ask for the Luna Hotel," Joe advised us when he dropped us, "that's been taken over by the Army and they'll look after you." We jumped aboard a ferry and were dropped right outside the Hotel.

"Well," said the sergeant at the reception desk, "I'm not supposed to take anyone without a chit from the Town Major."

"Just lead us to him," said Freda.

He suggested we tried 'phoning as it was getting late but we were told the Town Major would have to see us himself and he wouldn't be there again till next morning.

"All right," said the smiling sergeant, "I'll give you a room for tonight but to-morrow you must bring me the chit from the Town Major."

We promised faithfully we would. Mind you, had we known what kind of a man we were to confront, we wouldn't have slept nearly as well as we did in that luxurious room, in those luxurious beds, in that luxurious hotel. And all for two shillings.

We hadn't a worry in our minds next morning when we set out for the Town Major's office. Freda could be quite strict when she wanted to be. I was all for having a look at St. Mark's Square first but she wouldn't allow it. The chit came first. We were ushered into his office at 9 a.m. We were quite used to the Army, in fact we had always had particularly good relations with them, so we weren't in the least concerned. That is, we weren't till we saw him.

"Get out of Venice!" he roared at us, going very red in the face, "Wrens aren't allowed here".

I had the reputation of being quite winning when I wanted to be, so I smiled very sweetly. "We've come an awfully long way," I told him, "Please do let us stay a little while".

I was very taken aback as it was unwritten law, code of honour and all that to treat Wrens like princesses. This certainly wasn't the royal handout.

"Now, look here," said Freda, "you can't do that. We're here now and whether you like it or not, you are responsible for us."

He got so red in the face he made me think of an evening dress I'd had made out of vivid red curtain material, which wasn't rationed, just before coming out here. It really had been quite a hit. Only being the kind of linen that was meant for making chair covers, it felt like a ton weight when I put it on.

But to get back to the Town Major, he was still shouting.

"Go to Mestre - that's outside my jurisdiction," he ordered.

"But, sir," I said, laying on the deference, "we just can't keep bothering you Army men to run us backwards and forwards to and from Mestre. It must be all of five miles from here."

"There won't be any backwards and forwards," he yelled. "You will not spend one night in Venice."

"But we have already," Freda informed him. "We spent last night here, as a matter of fact."

For some moments he seemed quite stunned. Then he drew a form towards him, signed it and gave it to us.

"I will give you till tomorrow morning to get out of Venice," he said.

We had never been so ill-treated by the Army before. We there and then decided to stay as long as we wished, or at least till our leave was up, and this was a very simple matter. Each morning we presented ourselves at the Major's outer office and asked the clerk to renew our permit. With the Major's signature on the first one, the clerk knew all was well and I think he quite looked forward to our visits each day. After all, there couldn't have been many Wrens in there in the ordinary way. We on the other hand never thought it wise to clutter up his office too much, just in case his boss happened to come in. But he never did.

Well, to cut a long story short so as not to bore you, I should say we spent a marvelous few days in Venice. The Cathedral windows were boarded up to protect them in case of bombs but you could go inside and into the Doges Palace. I saw things I never ever saw again. In fact, I was a little haunted by them. The sight of soldiers who perhaps not long before had been battling it out in the nightmare of Monte Cassino or fighting their way right up the length of Italy in the rain and mud, standing in awe in the middle of the St. Mark's Square, when St. Mark himself, given the chance, would have looked at them in awe. The sight of gondolas crammed with soldiers on leave, with great fat smiles on their faces, in a funny way made me want to cry. Cheshire cats had nothing on them.

I suppose I must be a pretty lucky person altogether, anyway I certainly was that leave, for what should happen to us but to be put at a table for dinner in the Hotel that very first night with two terrific chaps. One was a very tough Jewish man who came from Bechuanaland and he kind of took a shine to me. That may sound conceited but I suppose he must have as he kept on sending me silk stockings for months afterwards. And if you ever lived during the War, you'll know what silk stockings meant to a girl. He was a straight guy and, you may not believe me, but I still have a picture of him with his Boys, a detachment of "coloured" chaps whom he loved like a father.

It always amazes me how people of completely different backgrounds, education and personalities can get on so well together. Take Freda and me for example. She came from Ireland. I came from England. I worried about everything. She just didn't give a damn for anyone or anything. I guess she reckoned the very worst that could happen to her had happened already. I remember she told me WRNS HQ had sent her on indefinite leave home after she was shipwrecked but she was itching to get back into the fray and nagged them to send her overseas again. I bet if that had been me I'd have kept as far away from war as they could send me.

It was a bit like that with Dave and Andrew. They were real pals, yet no two men could have been more unalike. Andrew had been sent to

Venice by something called, I think, the Fine Arts Commission. Anyway, whatever its name was, he had to look at all the beaten up museums and places and decide what was important enough to be protected. We went with him a few times to help him make up his mind. No kidding, we really did go with him to a couple of small palaces and he walked us round Venice showing us the churches, the Fenice Theatre, the art galleries and the famous restaurants. He was terrific. Dave kept telling me what a clever chap old Andrew was. He admired him no end.

Well, the time came, of course, to start thinking about getting back to Caserta. The reception desk at the Luna had one of those plate glass tops and Freda hit on this brilliant idea of putting an advertisement under the glass. You know the kind of thing: Can anyone give a couple of Wrens a lift back to Caserta? Or even to Rome would do. Despite the fact that we decided to say right out this time we were Wrens, we never could escape the medical aura. A couple of doctors volunteered for the job. They had a car with an ambulance trailer. If you ever want to feel really ill, accept a hitch in an ambulance trailer. Talk about seasick, I've never felt so landsick in all my life.

There was a signal lying on my desk when we returned: Unidentified WRNS officers seen in St. Mark's Square. By accident, I dropped it in the waste paper basket. Nobody mentioned it to us, so we didn't say anything either.

All in all, my year in Italy was a great success. I went with Freda to Florence as well as Venice. We had had on our staff an officer who had been the Vice-Consul there before the war and he applied to go back when that area was clear of fighting. Before he went, he said to me, "If you ever visit Florence, get in touch." So I got in touch. He very kindly provided us with a guide to show us around that lovely city and invited us to have dinner with him at the British Consulate in Fiesole, on the outskirts of Florence.

When we arrived, we discovered he was entertaining some Italians also. The ladies looked very elegant. "Oh, lord," I muttered to Freda, "we look so scruffy!" Anthony must have heard me, for he said, "I bet you're pretty hot and tired. Would you like a shower?" We were therewith ushered into the house. The other guests had been sitting under a tree in a gorgeous garden. We emerged refreshed if not comparable with the Italians, we, of course, being in uniform. As I have already told you, my knowledge of Italian was negligible and I don't think Freda's was much better, so it was an enjoyable, if difficult, evening. As a matter of fact, it was the only time I met Italians socially in the whole time I was in Italy.

This reminds me of a time when I wanted to buy my Father a birthday card. A frequent companion in Caserta was a young Army lieutenant. He volunteered to help me. You wouldn't think I would need help with such a simple thing, would you? But it wasn't so simple. "Where do you think we can find one?" I asked Simon. " Let's get transport into Naples," he said. So off we went in search of a birthday card. Simon didn't believe in speaking any language other than English. So at the first shop we tried, he went straight up to the counter and asked, "May we see some birthday cards." This produced an answer in a torrent of Italian by the large lady behind the counter.

"Birthday card," he repeated. "Shall I try?" I asked. "No, leave it to me," he said, and broke into "Happy birthday to you". He didn't sing badly but all she could do was laugh, so we decided to try somewhere else. This time the shopkeeper called her husband. He emerged from the dark interior full of smiles. "You want?" he asked in English. "Oh, good," said Simon, "someone who speaks English. All we want is a birthday card." "You want?" he said again. "A birthday card," Simon said again. By this time I was in hysterics. Simon said, "You know, birthday cake, candles?" He produced his cigarette lighter, lit the non-existent candles and blew them out. "Ah! Candele!" smiled the delighted shopkeeper, whilst his wife produced a box of them. I snatched up a picture postcard which must have been in the shop since the previous war. It was of one of those Edwardian girls, you know the kind of thing I mean. She had a sort of yearning look on her face as she gazed into the distance and there were a couple of lines about her longing for Him. I sent it to my Father explaining it was the nearest thing to a birthday card I could find. After that I made a small collection of them and sent them to various people. I hope they liked them. I think they did.

I think Audrey was the first of my Wren friends to marry. From the time she met Dennis Robinson her fate was sealed. She no longer wanted to make up foursomes or accept invitations. She had been my closest friend from the time we met at Crosby Hall till she was transferred to Malta after about nine months in Italy. Her mother had written to me when she had told her parents about Dennis. She wanted to know how well I knew him and what my opinion was of him. I could only tell her I knew little about him but that he seemed a very pleasant young man. Audrey now lived in her own dream world and went around looking something like the Edwardian girl on the postcard! I can't remember whether she became engaged to Dennis before or after she moved to Malta but around this time she applied to be released from the WRNS.

And so it was that she returned to England some months before me and I missed her wedding of course, which upset me as she had been my best chum for about a year. She was her parents' only child. They lived in a large flat in Earls Court Square and that is where I visited her when I was also finally released from the Service some months' later.

Dennis had been studying architecture when he was called up into the Army but had not qualified. That is a very long course, seven years, I think, and he had only completed either one or two. So Audrey's parents suggested he joined her father in the family printing business. Audrey was pregnant and they were very anxious to find a home of their own. It was a difficult time as everyone seemed to be doing the same as they came out of the Services. But they found a charming little house at Amersham-on-the-Hill and that is where she gave birth to two more bouncing babies. She showed me how I could get from my house in Golders Green to hers in forty-five minutes which seemed pretty good to me although I didn't get there to see her very often as Leo was working very hard combining his work in the Army with that offered to him in the musical profession[22].

---

[22] Brenda eventually learned to drive in the mid-1950's. However, Leo (her husband) was usually using the car for work and particularly once he became free-lance in about 1959 Brenda's priority was to remain at home to answer the telephone and book his work into his diary - 24:7 very nearly.

Brenda - Caserta

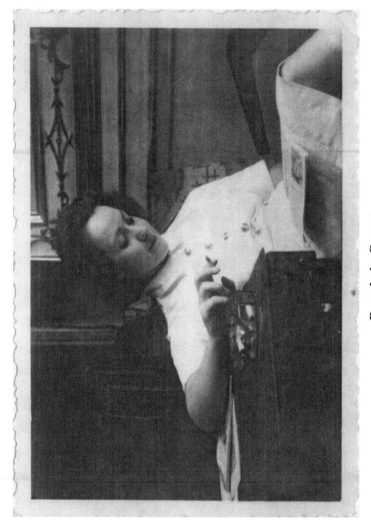

Brenda in Caserta

Brenda in Caserta

Brenda on Caserta Palace balcony

Brenda centre, Audrey Wilson right - Caserta

Brenda - reverse stamped "Napoli"

Brenda getting into the NOIC's car in Italy with Audrey Wilson to go to Villa Emma 16.6.45

Palace gardens Caserta

Richard II in palace theatre Caserta - Brenda front left

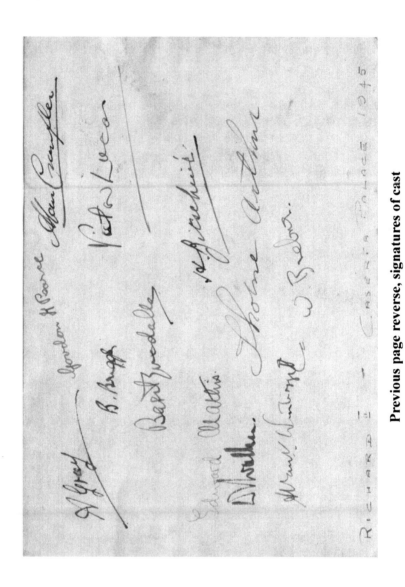

Previous page reverse, signatures of cast

Richard II in palace theatre Caserta - Brenda front centre

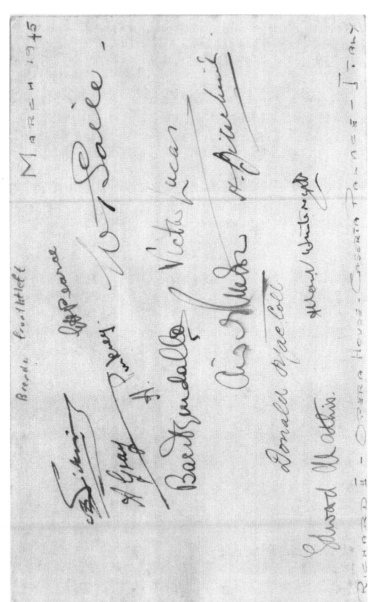

Previous page reverse, signatures of cast

Brenda 2nd row, 2nd from left - Caserta

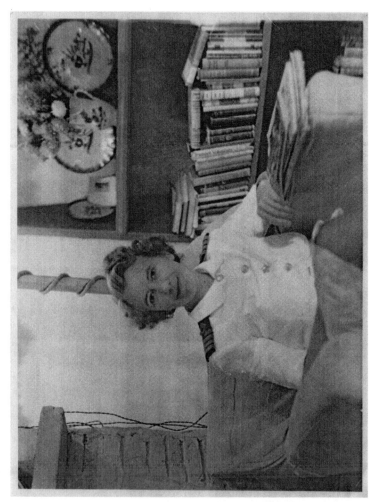

Supt Isherwood

5. Malta 1945[23]

At last the fighting was over, at least in Europe, for there was still no peace with Japan. On the official VE Day we, the Wrens, were told we should not go out alone in case there was trouble. We should at least walk in twos even to and from the Palace and our quarters. But all was quiet, no festivities nor demonstrations as far as we could see - certainly not here at Caserta.

Mussolini's fate had been sealed on 25th April when he had decided to disband what remained of his armed forces. He had attached himself to a small German convoy on its way to the Swiss frontier. On its way the party was confronted by Italian Partisans and next day Mussolini and his mistress were shot and hung for all to see in a square where Partisans had been recently shot.

As far as Hitler was concerned, I remember SO(1) explaining to me that preparations had to be made to forestall his retreat into a Redoubt in the Bavarian Alps. But he abandoned that idea and decided to remain in Berlin. Within two days of this decision Berlin was surrounded by the Russians. As everyone knows, Hitler shot himself.

Now the talk was of our leaving Italy for Malta, still part of the British Empire and the traditional headquarters of the British Navy in the Mediterranean. Most of us didn't want to go. We loved Italy and all our friends there. But most of our friends were either being re-appointed elsewhere or returning to the U.K. prior to being released. Some had gone ahead of us to Malta, but the main body of the Headquarters were flown out on the same day. As luck would have it, that day, in June I think, produced one of those violent electric storms. We all thought the operation would be cancelled but no such luck. It was too big an operation for that.

I had never flown before and was trying to hide my fear. The planes were not pressurised and the headache I set out with became gradually worse as I started to feel sick. I tried to think of other things: the Italian girls who cleaned and waited at table had gathered together to wave us goodbye and were in tears when the moment arrived. They were supposed

---

[23] Service record states that Brenda was at HMS St Angelo, Station Mediterranean 26 September 1945 - 24 December 1945.

71

to have been the Enemy, I thought. Was it that women found it impossible to hate each other? Or was it that we were aware that neither they nor we had started the War and felt no bitterness towards each other? And yet I don't think we felt the same about the Germans.

To my great relief we eventually put down in Malta. I remembered how much we had wanted to go ashore when we had been anchored some way out to allow one or two passengers to land on our original journey out. Looking around me at the burnt landscape, it didn't seem too promising. However, my spirits rose when we were taken to our new quarters. Mary Quarry had been appointed to Malta while I was in Italy and I was looking forward to seeing her again. Unfortunately, she was quartered in Whitehall Mansions in Msida and I was in the Imperial Hotel in Sliema. On top of that I was working in Fort St Elmo and she in Fort St Angelo. So we never bumped into each other casually but did manage to meet up by arrangement. (Audrey by this time had been released from the Service and returned to London to marry Dennis Robinson.) The powers that be had given us the Imperial Hotel at Sliema. This was a relatively small Hotel, probably had been a private house at one time. To us it was luxury with its beautiful staircase and carpeted floors, set back from the sea, probably to shield it from the gales and storms of winter.

I would put Sliema as Malta's second town of importance, Valletta being the first and, of course, the capital. Each morning the ferry (bus) would arrive to take us into Valletta where I discovered I was to work at Fort St. Elmo. Very few people worked there, most being allocated to Fort St. Angelo. Our Intelligence section was down to three: SO(1), Martin and me. Martin and I shared an office, Patrick had one to himself. It seemed a strange sort of environment, all very ancient and as unlike the Palace at Caserta as it was possible to be. Mary Quarry, who had been my closest friend in Dover, was there, working at Fort St. Angelo on Rear Admiral Packer's staff. He was in charge of Malta and its environs, whereas our Admiral Sir John Cunningham was in charge of the whole of the Mediterranean.

I have to admit I looked on Malta with a jaundiced eye. I didn't like its barren countryside, nor its war ravaged towns. It had had a very hard time and I was sorry for it. But I just didn't want to be there. I knew it had been bombed unmercifully, consistently for about two years, but now all that was in the past I felt ill. I had been unwell, in fact, on and off the whole year I had been in Italy. Everyone had gyppy tummy from time to time. If we had all stayed away for it only about fifty per cent of the staff would have been on duty at any given time. But here it was different, even apart from the fact that the silly idiots called gyppy tummy Malta Dog.

Having sworn I would never fly anywhere again, Patrick, my boss, asked me to go on a small errand back to Caserta. I didn't know whether to be glad or sorry. It only entailed staying there for about twenty-four hours but it meant taking to the air. I wasn't in a position to refuse, so I went.

The flight was far better than the previous one. As a start the plane was pressurised and also we had a break of an hour in Catania in Sicily.

Anyway, upon arrival at the Palace I contacted Simon and arranged to have dinner with him. That left me more than enough time for my mission and I saw one or two old friends. But on the whole the place seemed almost deserted, which, of course, it was. It was rather like going back to an old house after having moved but before the new people have taken over. It is no longer yours and you still wonder if you have done the right thing to leave. There were a few ghosts, too.

Michal had been one of these and later she appeared at Caserta. There was always something slightly mysterious about her and she was never able satisfactorily to explain what had brought her here. I know she didn't like the SO(1) in Malta and possibly he asked for her to be replaced. This would not have been surprising as she was generally scruffy in appearance and a bit too fond of a tipple. Neither she nor I knew what she was meant to be doing in Caserta. She seemed to drift around the Intelligence section but was never available if something was found for her to do. I think she was living in the Naples Wrennery or maybe just using it as we were allowed to do. However, she seemed to want me as a companion when she went off on some of her escapades. As a pretty naive girl, I think I must have been flattered that this sophisticated woman should want me as a chum. She dragged me around to dinner parties which ended always in Michal being drunk and on one particular occasion when I had insisted on being provided with transport to take us home, she had refused to come. Next day I had a frantic telephone call from her asking me to extricate her from someone's villa on the outskirts of Naples. "I can't get out of here," she said. "He's gone off to his job and I've no transport." At that time there were no taxis. I finally managed to get her friend, John, to organise a car but as far as I was concerned, this was the end. Already a complaint about her had gone to our Superintendent WRNS. As a result of this she was given a severe telling off and she in her turn wrote a short story which she gave me to read - entitled "Driftwood" - and which she sent to our Superintendent. Talk about a sob story...

Simon told me he was returning home at the end of the week. The journey would be mainly by train, which he anticipated being packed to overflowing.

Back in Malta, I discovered we had all been invited to a ball which was being given by the Governor at the Palace of the Grand Masters. Everyone was in a tizzy about what to wear. I had a length of light weight curtain material which I had brought away with me in case of need. My favourite evening dress, or I should say my only one, I had worn to death, so I decided this was the moment to find a dressmaker. There wasn't too much time, so I chose the first one recommended to me, a French lady. This turned out to be quite a different sort of fitting from those I had had in Caserta. I knew quite a bit of French but she, in fact, spoke English and there was no audience of friends or family. In the meantime, we all received written instructions not to buy long gloves as the wearing of these had been waived for the evening!!!

The dress turned out quite well and Hilda Jones and I were invited to dinner before the ball by Rear Admiral Packer and his wife. Joy Packer was quite well known as a writer, although, unfortunately at that time I hadn't read any of her books. I found myself partnered with a General, a real old stick in the mud with whom it was extremely difficult to talk. When I discovered I was to ride to the Palace with him in his car, I decided I would have to ditch him as soon as possible. Crowds of people stood around the Palace gates to watch as we were driven into the courtyard. The hall was impressive with its medieval men in armour ranged on either side and it was not too difficult to lose the General after a short time. Maybe he had decided to lose me. I now think the ball must have been to celebrate the end of the War.

One thing I must say about Malta and that is that it had a marvelous bus service, antiquated in the extreme, but going everywhere. I visited the ancient city of Mdina, the Silent City, wandered round its streets, had coffee on a balcony overlooking the countryside; saw the cathedral in Mosta where a bomb had come right through the roof without exploding and had been preserved, and treasured even, as a miracle. I realised Valetta had some beautiful old buildings and I sat in the Upper Barracca Gardens and looked out at the amazing view of the harbour and forts.

But I didn't feel well and I finally took the mistaken step of seeing the doctor. He immediately put me into sick bay. It was the beginning of December and distinctly chilly. The room was heated by a coal fire which was set and lit each morning. However often the patients told the cleaners how to do it, they always started with the coal and ended up with the paper. So, of course, we were obliged to do it ourselves. Really, Malta can get quite cold in the winter, at least in the evenings. Then one day I received notification that I was to travel back to the U.K. on Christmas Eve to be discharged from the WRNS. I was delighted but was told in sick bay I would have to sign a statement to the effect that I was well. At this point I was prepared to do almost anything to get back home, so I signed. A few days before our departure I was told I would be in charge of about eight Wrens.

Mary Quarry came to see me off and stood with me for several hours awaiting the tug to take us out to the SS. Britannic. There were two second officers in the group (I was but a miserable third), so I enquired why neither of them was in charge. "Oh, we haven't been well," came the prompt answer. More on the beam than I was, I thought. Once aboard all officers in charge of contingents were summoned to a meeting in the Captain's cabin where we were told that in view of the fact that we had many civilians aboard, there would be no celebration of Christmas, other than beer for the ratings and other drinks for the officers on Christmas Day. We all knew this was likely to cause trouble. Apart from the civilians, who were mainly wives of seamen stationed in Malta, there were other services also.

I soon discovered I had a very pregnant Wren in my group. What on earth do I do about this, I wondered. I was quite out of my depth, so I told her she must report to the Medical Officer on board as soon as possible and not to hesitate to ask to see him at any time she felt unwell. I frequently checked with her that she had done this.

At the meeting in the Captain's office I had been asked to do the rounds of the ship each morning with a naval lieutenant while everyone else was at lifeboat drill. I accepted no excuse to be absent from this from my Wrens. I was learning to put on an air of authority which seemed to get things done. To my horror I found the cabins occupied by civilians were just that, occupied. "Why aren't you at lifeboat drill?" I asked, glancing at the washing hanging on an improvised line across the cabin and the women lounging on the bunks A torrent of Maltese was then let loose of which we understood not a word. "Does anyone speak English?" I asked, not knowing there were few Maltese who did not. My companion, the lieutenant, shrugged his shoulders "What can you do?" he said. This occurred every morning.

On Boxing Day, a couple of days after we set sail, we were recalled to the Captain's office and informed the NOIC (Naval Officer-in-Charge) at one of the ports north of Naples was coming aboard next morning to speak to us. "I want you to assemble your groups on the upper deck at that time as he wishes to speak to all naval personnel". When we reached the appointed deck it was full of men in uniform, orders were being shouted and in no time squads were formed. I was asked to place the Wrens next to the Marines, famous for their smartness and efficiency. My heart sank but I called a petty officer and said, "Look, I know nothing about squad drill. I would like to put you in charge of it." "I've never done any, Ma'am," she replied. Oh God, I thought, just my luck. I said to my girls, "Just line up in rows and stand to attention." I felt very ashamed of myself but it was too late to regret all my years of squad drill avoidance. All around us orders were being shouted by Regimental Sergeant Majors or whatever, and then the chap in charge yelled at his squad that he wanted the Marines to change places with the WRNS. The Marine Sergeant shouted his orders, his men clicked to attention as each was expounded and I could see any moment these clockwork men might mow us down. "Girls," I said, " would you just change places with the men." And they did. A large box or something was put in place and the NOIC mounted it. He looked around the squads at attention before him and then said, "I don't think it necessary for the WRNS to remain".

I think the trouble had been all about the lack of Christmas celebrations and the poor NOIC had been called upon to calm things down.

6. Invalided out - 1946

I arrived home feeling ill and depressed. Well, not exactly home: we put in at Glasgow. I had come straight out of sick bay in Malta, hardly ready to take care of eight possibly difficult Wrens. I made up my mind once we put in at Glasgow my group could take care of themselves and I hastened to get a train to London. I know this was wrong but there were Wrens in Glasgow and it was their duty, I felt, to take care of us. It couldn't have been very pleasant for my parents as I think I was more depressed than I have ever been before or since. I felt isolated. For the last four and a half years I had been surrounded by friends. I had to appear in about ten days' time at a little hospital in Vincent Square for what I think was called a "release medical". My Mother was worried about me but I assured her I would get some pills from whichever doctor carried out this examination which would put me right.

It must have been very disappointing for my parents who wanted to hear about everything whilst I wanted nothing more than to be left in bed. I received a date and place to present myself for a release medical examination. This was at a small hospital in Westminster which had been taken over at some time as a sick bay for Wrens. I saw a very pleasant woman doctor. I told her about my gyppy tummy and asked her for some sulphur guanidine to clear it up. This was what was provided in the Mediterranean but she refused to give it to me.

"Go home, pack a bag and come straight back," she said. "I can't provide medication until I know exactly what is the matter with you."

Of course she was right but I went home determined not to return. But my Mother persuaded me and by that evening I was in a room for two in the sick bay.

Well, to cut a long story short, the doctors there, after several weeks, could not decide what was the matter with me, refusing to accept my assertion that it was just gyppy tummy. Then one day they popped me into a taxi and sent me round to see Sir Philip Manson-Bahr in Harley Street. He specialised in tropical illnesses, I was told. He was an elderly man (or so I thought then when he had probably barely touched seventy) who, after a prolonged examination, told me I had ulcerative colitis.

"I've never heard of it," I told him. "Never mind," he said, "You can go back to the sick bay. I shall lay down your treatment and you can invalided out of the WRNS."

"That won't be necessary," I told him, "I am due for discharge anyway."

"I shall insist you are invalided out," he replied.

In the mean time I must return to Vincent Square, the small hospital near Victoria Station, and he would lay down the treatment I was to have.

Three months were to pass before I was discharged from that sick bay and another six from the WRNS. I came ashore with no flags flying.

And so it was but not for many, many months.

It took three months to clear up the colitis and many friends who lived or happened to be in London during that time came to see me. Leo, my musician friend, was one of them and was very attentive. He was still in the Band of the Coldstream Guards and they didn't want to let him go. They had what they called a "string band" as well as the usual military band in which he played - or as he always said "pretended" to play the clarinet. But they were stationed in London and he managed to squeeze in a visit to me fairly often. Mary Quarry, from Dover and Malta came. My school friend Estelle Richenberg came, Sheila Forsyth one of my Dover friends and those who lived too far away wrote to me, including Patrick Barrow-Green, my boss in Italy and Malta. I began to cheer up.

I particularly remember Sylvia Priestley came because she tried to help me about what I was going to do eventually. Sylvia had been a dispatch rider in the WRNS - one who was constantly falling off her motor bike! She asked me if I would be interested in becoming secretary to an author named Robert Henriques who lived beneath them in the Albany, off Piccadilly.

"I would," I said "but I haven't the faintest idea when I will be coming out of here."

"Never mind, I'll tell him that. In case you were interested I brought along two or three of his books for you to read."

I was quite overwhelmed by her kindness but nothing came of it in the end, mainly due to the fact that he wanted me to spend most of the time at his house in the country and I was still in no mood to suffer isolation of any sort. However, it gave me the opportunity to see inside this historic block of flats when I later I visited him and the Priestleys.

Sylvia's father, J. B. Priestley, had always been a hero of mine but I'm afraid I was struck dumb by the honour of meeting him. Mrs. Priestley, ex-Mrs. Wyndham Lewis, was charming to me and I was later included in a party they were giving, when I spent the night in one of the Albany's guest rooms.

Home once again after three months in hospital, I was told I must not work for at least six months. It was enjoyable to see old friends once again but they were mainly occupied in one way or another whereas time was heavy on my hands. Coming back from town one day, I started thinking of the miniature opera house in the Palace at Caserta. There various groups had put on plays from time to time, including the Americans who performed "Our Town" by Thornton Wilder while the latter was at Caserta and able to advise them. The RAF were doing Richard II, except that they had no women and put out an SOS for volunteers. I landed up with the part of Queen to Richard. There were one or two professionals in the cast, including, I think, Richard himself, and it gave me enormous pleasure to work with them. It was quite a success, although perhaps not the right choice for the circumstances. As far as I was concerned, it had taken up far too much time and sometimes I found myself running from our office to rehearsals and back again to catch up with work I had had to leave. They intended to follow it up with the dramatic version of Peer Gynt but I decided not to take part.

Audrey had had a baby. She and Dennis were temporarily living with her parents in Earls Court Square and I went round to see their gorgeous son and heir, John. He was so chubby and sweet and Audrey so efficient, as she was in most things. But this took one afternoon. What was I to do with the rest of the time?

Well, I was thinking of all this on top of the bus and when we arrived at Swiss Cottage I just got off and walked up to the Embassy Theatre which was just across the road. Walking through the stage door, I asked where I would find the stage manager. When he was pointed out to me, I asked if he could do with some help.

"Would you be interested in being an assistant stage manager?" Shaun Sutton asked me. "No pay, I'm afraid."

From that time on I was his dog's body, running hither and thither, setting up the stage before the curtain went up, exchanging furniture between acts, and so on. There were two or three of us unpaid assistants. I found it hard, working practically every day of the week, including Sundays, paying bus fares and various incidentals, like coffees, in their club, and receiving not a penny in return. But I enjoyed watching how the actors approached their parts. They were mostly very friendly, Henry Oscar, well known in his day, refusing to start a rehearsal until I had kissed him good morning! For the next three months I worked myself to death, Sundays as well, but because I wasn't paid I didn't consider it the kind of work I had been told not to do. I worked almost as hard as I had in the WRNS and quite enjoyed it. But it wasn't exactly a rest cure. At Christmas, when, incidentally, my name was included on the programme, Leo asked me if his nephew, Ivan, could watch a rehearsal. We had a small orchestra for this Christmas play and some of the chaps knew Leo and teased me about him. I had been promised a paid job in the New Year in their other theatre in Buxton but the weather turned so cold they closed that theatre.

I thought I had finished with the Navy when I was finally discharged from the WRNS when I left hospital. However, whilst working at the Embassy Theatre I received a message from one of the staff there. My instructions on leaving hospital were that I should not work for 6 months. However, after a while I received a message from Admiral Cunningham's ex-secretary that she was giving up a job as secretary to the Admiral in charge of U.S. Forces in Europe and I might possibly be interested in taking it on. I went along to their headquarters in Grosvenor Square and was accepted immediately. It was all very impressive, in particular the magnificent office I would share with the Admiral's Flag Lieutenant, my desk being next to a window overlooking the Square.

My work mainly dealt with the Admiral Connolly's social life. He had to give parties of all kinds, cocktail, dinner, lunch, etc. and formal invitations had to be sent to many titled and high ranking people. I got the impression that he did it only because it was part of his job and he would have preferred to stick to just the serious side of his work. However, he had the wrong person for this as I didn't mix with titled people and had no idea how they should be addressed! I had all the standard tomes on the floor next to my desk but couldn't follow them, or maybe I just was insufficiently interested.

I have never regretted joining the WRNS but the fact remains that I was very unwell when I came out and ended up in hospital for several months. Later I ended up in a hospital in Roehampton - known for its skill in making artificial limbs. As I didn't require any artificial limbs I wondered why I was there but as time went on I came to the conclusion that they associated the limbless with anything caused by the war.

Looking back over what I have written about the friends I made in the WRNS it amounts to very little. And yet they meant so much to me. In my early days in Dover at HMS "Wasp" Mary Quarry[24] and Sheila Forsyth became my friends and this friendship lasted for life - as did Audrey Wilson[25]. Sadly, Sheila passed away about two years ago[26].

---

[24] Mary Scott née Quarry died 15th September 2010 in Chichester.
[25] Audrey Robinson née Wilson I believe died in or near Aldeburgh prior to 2000.
[26] Sheila Turner née Forsyth probably died 2005-2010, estimated from when this was probably written.

3rd Officer Brenda Heimann

Brenda in her officer's uniform

Postscript

In case you were wondering, Brenda did marry viola player Leo Birnbaum in April 1947. By then, as her mother was worried just after the War that once again Brenda would have a German Jewish name, Leo had changed his name by Deed Poll to Birney. Two years later, I, their only child, was born.

Their home was at 49, Hodford Road, Golders Green for all but the first couple of years of their marriage when they rented a house next door to Brenda's parents. (There was a terrible shortage of housing in London in the decade or so after the 2nd World War as a result of all the bombing.)

Her life was completely focused upon being a musician's wife and mother until the mid/late 1960s when Brenda became a part-time Home and Hospital Tutor for the Inner London Education Authority. Later she was asked also, by her pre-war friend Nina Snook née Sadler (from Industrial Engineering) to represent her very smart porcelain shop at auction houses, bidding for the finest Victorian and Edwardian pieces on behalf of Leather & Snook in Piccadilly. Both very part-time jobs came to an end eventually - I suppose when Brenda was in her mid-70s. Sadly even now, approaching her 99th birthday, that gyppy tummy which seems to have started during the strain and hard conditions of working on the Invasion of Normandy - and then in Italy and in Malta - during her twenties, still rears its ugly head from time to time as ulcerative colitis. She is a War Pensioner.

A few months ago my mother received a letter from the Wrens Association asking for recollections of her time in the Service. They were writing to all ex-Wrens born in 1917, the year the WRNS was founded. I promised to try and piece these memoirs together and thought that were I to publish this section of her life in its entirety, it would make a very good 99th birthday present.

Hazel Dakers, June 2016

Lightning Source UK Ltd.
Milton Keynes UK
UKOW02f1831081116
287183UK00001B/282/P